*Everyman, I will go with thee,
and be thy guide*

'Mark Rutherford'
William Hale White

CLARA HOPGOOD

Edited by
LORRAINE DAVIES
Liverpool Hope University College

EVERYMAN
J. M. DENT · LONDON
CHARLES E. TUTTLE
VERMONT

This edition first published by Everyman Paperbacks in 1996

Introduction and other critical apparatus © J. M. Dent 1996

J. M. Dent
Orion Publishing Group
Orion House
5 Upper St Martin's Lane
London WC2H 9EA
and
Charles E. Tuttle Co. Inc.
28 South Main Street
Rutland, Vermont 05701, USA

Typeset in Sabon by CentraCet Limited, Cambridge
Printed in Great Britain by
The Guernsey Press Co. Ltd, Guernsey, C. I.

British Library Cataloguing-in-Publication Data is available
upon request.

ISBN 0 460 87771 2

CONTENTS

NOTE ON THE AUTHOR AND EDITOR

MARK RUTHERFORD is the pseudonym of William Hale White (1831–1913). Hale White was born into a family of devout Dissenters who lived at Bedford and claimed to trace their ancestors back to Cromwell's army. In 1852, shortly after he had commenced his studies in a Dissenting theological college, Hale White was expelled for heresy. The expulsion was something of a *cause célèbre* and drew to Hale White's defence eminent Christian Socialists like F. D. Maurice and Charles Kingsley. After leaving the college Hale White went on to pursue a successful career as a civil servant in the Admiralty. In his spare time he produced a large volume of journalism, translations of Spinoza's *Ethic* and *Tractatus*, and the six novels of Mark Rutherford.

LORRAINE DAVIES is lecturer in English Literature at Liverpool Hope University College.

CHRONOLOGY OF HALE WHITE'S LIFE

Year   Age   Life

1831   Born 22 December in Bedford, son of William and Mary
              White

CHRONOLOGY OF HIS TIMES

Year	Literary Context	Historical Events
1797–1815		Napoleonic Wars. Revolutionary turmoil in Europe. Radicalism and repression in Britain
1815		Corn Law prohibits import of foreign wheat until the domestic price reaches 80 shillings (£4) a quarter
1828		Test and Corporation Acts repealed
1829		Roman Catholic Relief Act places Catholics on same footing as Noncomformists
1829–32		Radical banker Thomas Attwood forms the 'General Political Union between the Lower and the Middle Classes of the People'
1830–33	Lyell, *Principles of Geology*	
1831		8 October, First Reform Bill rejected in Britain; Parliament dissolved and new Parliament elected with majority for reform; Mazzini addresses appeal for Italian independence and is exiled
1832		7 June, First Reform Act passed; Mazzini expelled from France
1833		First Factory Act

Year   Age   Life

1840   8   Enters English School, Angel Street, Bedford

Year	Literary Context	Historical Events
1834		Poor Law Amendment Act; Tolpuddle Martyrs victimised; Mazzini organises abortive invasion of Savoy; Abolition of Slave Trade
1835	David Friedrich Strauss, *Das Leben Jesu, kritisch bearbeitet* (The Life of Jesus, critically examined)	
1836	Carlyle, *Sartor Resartus*	
1836–7		Activity of London Working Mens' Association; Mazzini banished from Switzerland
1837	Carlyle, *The French Revolution*	Accession of Queen Victoria; Mazzini takes refuge in London
1838	Hennel, *An Enquiry into the Origins of Christianity*	Anti-Corn Law League founded
1839	Carlyle, *Chartism*	First climax of Chartism at height of trade depression
1840	Birth of Thomas Hardy	Formation of National Charter Association
1841	Carlyle, *On Heroes, Hero-worship and the Heroic in History*; *Punch* founded	
1842	Wordsworth, *Poems* Tennyson, *Poems*	Second peak of Chartist activity
1843	Carlyle, *Past and Present* First volume of Ruskin's *Modern Painters*, four subsequent volumes published in 1846, 1856 (vols III and IV), and 1860 Mill, *System of Logic*	
1844	*Vestiges of the Natural History of Creation*, attributed to Robert Chambers, published anonymously after his death	
1845		Newman joins Church of Rome

Year	Age	Life
1846	14	Leaves English School
1847	15	Father closely involved in general election, supporting Whig Lord Charles Russell, who is returned as Member for the County
1848	16	February, admitted to membership in the Old Meeting (later known as the Bunyan Meeting), Bedford. Autumn, matriculates at Countess of Huntingdon's College
1849	17	Meets Caleb Morris
1851	19	October, transfers to New College, St John's Wood, London
1852	20	March, expelled from New College with two other students for questioning the authority of the Scriptures. Autumn, appointed schoolmaster in Stoke Newington but quickly abandons the position; begins working for the publisher John Chapman in London, where he meets Marian Evans (George Eliot) who also works there
1854	22	February, leaves Chapman's; becomes clerk in Registrar General's Office, Somerset House, London. 19 October, father speaks at a meeting of the Literary Institution in Bedford attended by Lords Charles and John Russell. In November he accepts the post of Assistant Doorkeeper at the House of Commons, an appointment in the gift of Charles Russell

Year	Literary Context	Historical Events
1846	The Brontës, *Poems* *The Life of Jesus* (*Leben Jesu*), trsl. George Eliot	Repeal of Corn Laws; Potato Famine in Ireland; National Charter conference in Leeds
1847	Charlotte Brontë, *Jane Eyre* Emily Brontë, *Wuthering Heights* Dickens, *Dombey and Son*	
1848	Elizabeth Gaskell, *Mary Barton* Marx and Engels, *The Communist Manifesto* Mill, *Principals of Political Economy* Millais, D. G. Rossetti and Holman Hunt found the Pre-Raphaelite Brotherhood	Democratic revolutions in Europe; Last flare up of Chartism
1849	Froude, *The Nemises of Faith*	Mazzini received enthusiastically in Leghorn; Roman Republic declared dead; French arrive in Rome, the republic falls
1850	Death of Wordsworth Wordsworth, *The Prelude* Tennyson, *In Memoriam*; becomes Poet Laureate	Roman Catholic hierarchy established in Britain
1851	Carlyle, *The Life of John Sterling*, preface by WHW Spencer, 'The Development Hypothesis'	Napoleon III assumes power in France; The Great Exhibition
1852	Florence Nightingale, *Cassandra*	
1854	Tennyson, *The Charge of the Light Brigade*	Crimean War declared by Britain and France against Russia; Florence Nightingale leads nursing team to Scutari; Gold Rush in Australia

Year	Age	Life
1855	23	January, parents move to London, his father takes up his post in the House of Commons
1856	24	29 March, Caleb Morris leaves London for his native Wales. 22 December, marries Harriet Arthur in Kentish Town Congregational Church
1857	25	12 March, becomes Registrar of Births and Deaths, Marylebone whilst continuing to work at Somerset House
1858	27	December, appointed to clerkship in Accountant General's Department at the Admiralty. 6 March, 'Births, Deaths, and Marriages', *Chambers Magazine*
1860	28	Visits Germany
1861	29	Summer, begins to contribute 'Metropolitan Notes' to *Aberdeen Herald*, these appear every Saturday from 11 May 1861 to 27 January 1872. October, birth of son John Harry
1862	30	Spring, moves to Carshalton, Surrey
1865	33	Becomes Parliamentary Correspondent to the *Morning Star*, London: 'Below the Gangway' features every Monday from 13 February 1865 to 10 July 1865. October, moves to Epsom

Year	Literary Context	Historical Events
1855	Browning, *Men and Women* Tennyson, *Maud* Trollope, *The Warden*	
1856		Crimean War ends; Feminist campaign for Married Women's Property Act
1857	Elizabeth Barrett Browning, *Aurora Leigh* Elizabeth Gaskell, *The Life of Charlotte Brontë*	
1858	Carlyle, *Frederick the Great*	
1859	Arnold, *England and the Italian Question* Darwin, *On the Origin of the Species by Natural Selection, or, the Preservation of Favoured Races in the Struggle for Life* Mill, *On Liberty* Smiles, *Self Help*	Suez Canal begun
1860		Unification of Italy
1861	Arnold, *On Translating Homer*	Only Rome remains outside united Italy; American Civil War begins; Death of Prince Albert
1862	Colenso, *The Pentateuch and the book of Joshua critically examined*	Garibaldi attempts to seize Rome; Bismarck comes to power in Prussia
1863	Elizabeth Gaskell, *Sylvia's Lovers* Mill, *Utilitarianism*	
1864	Newman, *Apologia Pro Vita Sua* Trollope, *Can You Forgive Her?*	
1865	Lecky, *History of the Rise and Influence of the Spirit of Rationalism in Europe*	Death of Richard Cobden; American Civil War ends

Year	Age	Life
1866	34	3 February, begins to contribute 'Sketches in Parliament' to the *Birmingham Daily Post and Journal*, until 31 January 1880. March, *An Argument for the extension of the Franchise* (pamphlet) published. 17 April, birth of son Earnest Victor
1867	35	Moves to Isleworth. 19 January, begins to write 'Letters by a Radical' for the *Rochdale Observer*, appears every Saturday until 30 March 1872
1868	36	Moves to Park Hill, Carshalton. 21 March, visits Thomas Carlyle with his father
1869	37	Transferred to Purchase Department in the Admiralty. 14 December, birth of twins Earnest Theodore and Mary Theodora
1872	40	14 February, begins occasional contributions: 'Sketches in Parliament' and 'How it Strikes a Stranger', to the *Nonconformist*, until 6 August 1873. 2 March, 'Our London Letter' first printed in the *Norfolk News*, continues until 17 March 1883
1873	41	Begins to write 'London Letter' for the *Scotsman*
1879	47	15 May, visits Robert Browning

Year	Literary Context	Historical Events
1866	Arnold, *Essays in Criticism* Kingsley, *The Water Babies*	Reform Bill drafted by Gladstone; Venice secured for Italy; Mill petitions Parliament for women's vote
1867	Marx, *Das Kapital*, first vol	Second Reform Bill by Disraeli
1869	Arnold, *Culture and Anarchy* Mill, *On the Subjection of Women*	
1870	Death of Dickens	Franco-Prussian War begins; Elementary Education Act; Married Women's Property Act
1871	George Eliot, *Middlemarch* Darwin, *The Descent of Man and Selection in Relation to Sex*	Trades Unions legal; Rome and Papal States annexed to kingdom of Italy; University Test Act
1872	Butler, *Erewhon*, published anonymously George Eliot, *Middlemarch*	Death of Mazzini at Pisa; Voting by Secret Ballot; Edison's invention of the telegraph
1873	Arnold, *Literature and Dogma* Mill, *Autobiography* Pater, *Studies in the History of the Renaissance*	
1874	Hardy, *Far from the Madding Crowd*	
1876	George Eliot, *Daniel Deronda*	Queen Victoria proclaimed Empress of India; University entrance and medical education opened to British women
1877	Ibsen, *The Pillars of Society*	
1878	Hardy, *The Return of the Native*	
1879	Ibsen, *A Doll's House*	

Year	Age	Life
1881	49	4 March, *The Autobiography of Mark Rutherford: Dissenting Minister*. 22 June, pays a second visit to Robert Browning. December, 'The Mysterious Portrait' (short story) published in the *Birmingham Daily Post* (later included in *Mark Rutherford's Deliverance*)
1882	50	Death of father
1883	51	May, translation of Spinoza's *Ethic* published in Hale White's own name. July–August, visits Germany
1885	53	2 January, *Mark Rutherford's Deliverance: Being the Second Part of his Autobiography*. 28 November, writes to the *Athenaeum* to protest that J. W. Cross's *Life* of George Eliot obliterates Eliot's qualities by making her too 'respectable'
1887	55	9 March, *The Revolution in Tanner's Lane*
1889	57	February, moves to Street Farm, Ashstead
1890	58	June, *Miriam's Schooling*
1891	59	Death of wife from disseminated sclerosis, having been ill for more than thirty years
1892	60	21 March, retires from the Admiralty after completing 33 years' service
1893	61	December, *Catharine Furze*
1894	62	Revised edition of *Ethic* published
1895	63	March, translation of Spinoza's *Tractatus de Intellectus Emendatione* in Hale White's name
1896	64	March, *Clara Hopgood*. 4 July, 'Spinoza's Doctrine of the Relationship between Mind and Body' in *The International Journal of Ethics*

Year	Literary Context	Historical Events
1880	Death of George Eliot	
1881	Death of Carlyle	
	James, *The Portrait of a Lady*	
1882		Death of Darwin
1883	Schreiner, *The Story of an African Farm*	
1884	Jones, 'The Breaking of a Butterfly', founded on Ibsen's Nora, produced at The Prince of Wales Theatre, London	Third Reform Bill
1885		Age of sexual consent raised to 16; Foundation of Socialist League demonstrations against employment in London
1886	James, *The Bostonians*	
1888	Death of Arnold	
	Ellis, *Women and Marriage*	
1889	Publication in English of Ibsen's *A Doll's House*	Death of John Bright
1890	Emily Dickinson, *Poems*	
	Gissing, *The Emancipated*	
1891	Hardy, *Tess of the d'Urbervilles*	Free elementary education
	Morris, *News from Nowhere*	
1892	Death of Thomas Cooper, Chartist	
1893	Gissing, *The Odd Women*	Foundation of Independent Labour Party
1894	Moore, *Esther Waters*	Woman Suffrage Act in New Zealand
1895	Freud, *Studies in Hysteria*	Trial of Oscar Wilde
	Hardy, *Jude the Obscure*	
1896	Death of Morris	

Year	Age	Life
1897	65	31 May, *A Description of the Wordsworth and Coleridge Manuscripts in the possession of Mr T. Norton Longman*, edited by WHW
1899	67	8 May, moves to Crowborough, Tunbridge Wells. July, edition of Coleridge's poems: *A Facsimile Reproduction of the Proofs and MSS. of Some of the Poems*, edited by James Dykes Campbell with preface and notes by WHW
1900	68	December, *Pages from a Journal*
1901	69	4 January, letter 'The Author of Mark Rutherford on National Affairs', printed in *The Bedfordshire Times and Independent*
1902	70	August, 'George Eliot as I knew her', published in *The Bookman*, later printed in *Last Pages from a Journal*
1903	71	14 June, moves to Groombridge, Sussex
1904	72	October, *John Bunyan* (dated 1905 on title page)
1905	73	15 July, letter 'Trades Unionism in the Civil Services' in the *Spectator*
1907	75	March, *Selections from Dr Johnson's 'Rambler'*, edited with preface and notes by WHW. 26 November, Carlyle's *The Life of John Sterling*, introduction by WHW. Meets Dorothy Vernon Horace Smith, having invited her to visit him after reading her first novel, *Miss Mona*
1908	76	11 July, 'A Study in Overlooking', review of *Miss Mona*, in *The Nation*
1909	77	'Frank Burnet', review of Dorothy Vernon Horace Smith's second novel, in *The Nation*

Year	Literary Context	Historical Events
1897	Ellis, *Studies in the Psychology of Sex*	Tate Gallery opens in London; Queen Victoria's Diamond Jubilee
1898		Death of Gladstone
1899	Wilde, *The Importance of Being Earnest*	Boer War begins
1900	Conrad, *Lord Jim* Death of Ruskin Death of Wilde	Foundation of the Labour Representative Committee
1901		Death of Queen Victoria; Accession of Edward VII
1902	James, *The Wings of the Dove*	Boer War ends
1903		Emmeline Pankhurst founds the WSPU
1904	Conrad, *Nostromo*	
1905	Einstein, *Special Theory of Relativity* James, *The Golden Bowl*	
1906	Death of Ibsen	Labour Representation Committee wins 29 seats in General Election; changes its name to Labour Party; Movement for Women's Suffrage becomes active
1907	Dorothy Vernon Horace Smith, *Miss Mona* Synge, *The Aran Islands*	
1908	Forster, *A Room with a View*	
1909	Death of Swinburne Wells, *Ann Veronica* Dorothy Vernon Horace Smith, *Frank Burnet*	Old Age Pensions introduced in Britain

Year	Age	Life
1911	79	8 April, marries Dorothy Vernon Horace Smith, who is 45 years his junior
1913	81	14 March, dies at his home in Groombridge. 24 July, *The Early Life of Mark Rutherford (W. Hale White) By Himself*
1915		8 July, *Last Pages from a Journal*
1923		1 May, *Letters to Three Friends*

Year	Literary Context	Historical Events
1910	Forster, *Howards End*	Death of Florence Nightingale; Death of Edward VII; Accession of George V; First Post-Impressionist Exhibition; MPs paid for first time
1911	Lawrence, *The White Peacock* Dorothy Vernon Horace Smith, *Isabel*	
1913	Lawrence, *Sons and Lovers*	Hunger strikes by suffragettes
1924	*The Groombridge Diary*, ed. Dorothy Vernon White (née Horace Smith, WHW's second wife)	

INTRODUCTION

Mark Rutherford is the pseudonym of William Hale White who was born in 1831 into a family of Dissenters who lived at Bedford. William White, Hale White's father, was one of the leading members of the Bunyan Meeting and a popular lay preacher. A staunch democrat, William White had been involved in most of the political controversies that beset Bedford in the 1830s and 40s. In *The Early Life of Mark Rutherford*, a small volume of autobiographical notes written towards the end of his life, Hale White describes his family as 'Radical, and almost Republican'.[1] This radicalism derived from the traditional struggle of Dissenters to achieve equal status with members of the Church of England. The Test and Corporation Acts[2] had made it illegal for Dissenters to hold public office. Though the repeal of these acts in 1828 gave Nonconformists reason to hope that the discrimination they had suffered would soon be ended, in practice the removal of their disabilities was to take another decade. Dissenters like the Whites had a passionate interest in the movement for reform.

The background from which William Hale White's personality was formed was deeply religious, politically active and, above all, serious-minded. Two events in his youth seem to have been significant in determining the kind of man that he became and the type of fiction that Mark Rutherford was to write. The first was his 'conversion' in the Bunyan Meeting; the second, his expulsion, with two other students, from New College, London for heresy (Dissenters were excluded from the universities because of their refusal to give assent to the thirty-nine articles of the Church of England). His entry into theological college was conditional upon having experienced 'conversion' and yet Hale White came to realise that the 'experience' he had professed was really no more than a formality. The child of devout parents, his piety had been taken for granted, by himself no less than the congregation. He was expelled from college for questioning the inspiration of the Scriptures and the veracity of the Bible. The expulsion was really the culmination of the 'failed' conversion. It is this that makes Hale White's crisis of faith untypical of his age. He had not fallen from faith into doubt, but realised that he had had no faith of his own to begin with.

While he was at New College, struggling to come to terms with this sense of the emptiness of his belief, Hale White discovered Wordsworth, as does Mark Rutherford in the *Autobiography*. What Hale White found in the *Lyrical Ballads* 'modified' his belief by providing a means of escaping the 'concentration'[3] on self that his creed had encouraged. He was moved especially by the following lines from *Tintern Abbey*:

> Knowing that Nature never did betray
> The heart that loved her.

For both Rutherford and Hale White, Wordsworth's poems implied a 'living God', altogether different from the 'artificial God of the churches'.[4] The effect of Wordsworth thus links *The Early Life* to the early fiction. The use of nature as a means of escaping the self connects the factual *Early Life* to the fictional *Autobiography*, and beyond that to the other novels, culminating in *Clara Hopgood*. Hale White could see that it was 'Wordsworth and not German research' that precipitated his expulsion from New College. The *Lyrical Ballads* exposed a need to be free to decide for himself what he could believe, what was right and what was wrong. At the time of the New College controversy, William White published a pamphlet in defence of his son, entitled *To Think or not to Think*.[5] Clearly, 'to think' was to expose oneself to censure, to be faced with difficult choices, and yet it was the only way to cast off 'what was dead' and lay 'hold of what was true'.[6] It is this kind of thinking that the novels of Mark Rutherford as a whole enact, and never more uncompromisingly than in *Clara Hopgood*.

In the years that separate the failure of his early aspirations to become a minister from the publication of the first novels, Hale White established a successful career in the civil service. He began to contribute articles to numerous periodicals, married Harriet Arthur and saw the birth of his children. He came late to fiction (he was fifty when his first novel was published), but the ideas from which the fiction proceeds had had a lengthy gestation. The early novels, *The Autobiography of Mark Rutherford* and *Mark Rutherford's Deliverance*,[7] which in a sense 'relive' the troublesome years surrounding the New College controversy, are, as a result of this, the product of a mature mind reappraising the past from a safe distance in time. When it finally came, the impetus to write the early novels seems to have arisen from Hale White's need to confess or bear witness to his religious bewilderment more than from any desire for literary fame. The kind of confession that the first novels comprise is complex and distanced by the use of the fictional narrator.

Rutherford is not simply the 'double'[8] of William Hale White, not least because Rutherford experiences no such dramatic break with religious tradition as did his creator. Mark Rutherford is endowed with a mental and material life which, while reflecting Hale White's in its salient details, remains distinct in specifics. Readers of the earlier novels need to distinguish between Hale White and Rutherford in a way that we have no cause to in the case of Marian Evans and her pseudonym, George Eliot. Hale White felt that it was 'impossible' for anyone not 'gifted with Rousseau's shamelessness' to speak the truth about their self.[9] The distance between author and fictional self or persona in the *Autobiography* and *Deliverance* allows for both self-confession and self-analysis. Rutherford functions as a means by which Hale White can disclose those aspects of his autobiography that he felt were 'shameful'. At the same time however, Rutherford serves to show how it was the conjunction of a particularly morbid character with a creed that actively promoted introspection, rather than the creed alone, that is at the heart of Rutherford's failure to escape from the misery that crushes him.

A distinct alteration occurs in the relationship of Mark

Rutherford to William Hale White between the first novels and
the last. Many years after the publication of the *Autobiography*,
Hale White was to write that the idea that there was 'nothing in
the old creed worth retaining' was a mistake and that much
must be forgiven in Puritanism in view of the 'earnestness with
which it insists on the distinction between right and wrong'.[10]
Looking at the novels as a whole, it becomes clear that they
chart a movement away from the self-involvement of the *Autobiography* and *Deliverance* towards an analysis of the problem
of the distinction of right and wrong in a more inclusive sense.
The *Autobiography*, *Deliverance*, and *The Revolution in Tanner's Lane*[11] are about men who are born at the wrong time and
are forced to find some means of accommodating themselves to
the loss of orthodox faith. The fourth book, *Miriam's
Schooling*[12] begins from a different point to that of those which
precede it. Miriam is a kind of bridge between the characters of
Mark Rutherford and Zachariah Coleman[13] and the women
who are to come after her. She embodies the struggles of the
earlier protagonists in the sense that she too has to undergo
personal regeneration after disappointment, though in her case,
as in the novels that follow, in a secular form. At the same time,
she anticipates the later novels, *Catharine Furze*[14] and *Clara
Hopgood*, the concern of which is the experience of women
faced with difficult moral choices. The more closely one reads
Rutherford, the clearer it becomes that the novels develop out
of each other, addressing concerns previously established, but
always from a different perspective and an altered consciousness. The distance travelled between the first and the final novel
is considerable: only when we come to *Clara Hopgood* does the
distinction between Hale White and Mark Rutherford
disappear.

Clara Hopgood is the last of a group of highly individual
novels written by 'Mark Rutherford' in the 1880s and 90s.[15] In
spite of the praise that Mark Rutherford's writing had attracted
from contemporaries such as Matthew Arnold[16] and William
Dean Howells,[17] when the book was first published in 1896 its
reviews were not favourable. Some critics allowed that the novel

was not entirely without merit, but they saw what worth there was as being spoilt by an 'almost careless want of directness and unity in the mechanism'. Though it was rather grudgingly recognised as the 'work of an original thinker', *Clara Hopgood* was considered, at best, an 'inchoate mass of good material'.[18] But if the book was thought 'unsatisfactory' in style, it was deemed even more deficient in its 'moral teaching'; in short, according to W. Robertson Nicholl, it was 'unworthy' of its author 'from every point of view'.[19] What makes this last invective the more notable is that it comes from a man who had been one of the most ardent admirers of Rutherford's earlier novels.

This coolness on the part of contemporary reviewers is in marked contrast to the views of twentieth century critics. Irvin Stock has written of *Clara Hopgood* as 'the highest development of White's genius'.[20] John Lucas describes Rutherford's last novel as his 'finest'.[21] Writers like Andre Gide, D. H. Lawrence and George Orwell all wrote admiringly of Rutherford's singular prose style. But perhaps it is David Daiches who gives the strongest clue as to why so many of Rutherford's contemporaries failed to realise the true achievement of his work. The way in which Rutherford 'spells out kinds of social and religious concerns in an intimate and detailed way', thus giving 'a remarkable new psychological and ethical twist to an old Christian doctrine', makes him different from any 'other writer of his time', according to Daiches.[22] *Clara Hopgood* with its new form, modern ideas and intimate style, was simply too far ahead of its time to be easily appreciated by readers raised on the classic nineteenth century realist novel with its clear moral base and firm sense of closure.

The contemporary critical reception of *Clara Hopgood* had something in common with that accorded Thomas Hardy's *Jude the Obscure*, published a year earlier and similarly branded as 'immoral' and 'anti-marriage'. In her study of Thomas Hardy, Rosemarie Morgan writes how, having borne the attacks that *Tess of the D'Urbervilles* (1891) had provoked, Hardy hoped that *Jude* might be greeted by a more sympathetic readership.[23]

This uncharacteristic optimism on Hardy's part proved unfounded. The exclamation of one female reader that *Jude* exhibited a 'coarseness . . . beyond belief', was representative of the critical response to the book.[24] It was this kind of reaction that 'killed all interest' in Hardy for the novel as a form, and 'ended' his prose contributions to literature.[25]

Though both Hardy and Rutherford endured similar disapproval, and though neither went on to produce another novel after 1896,[26] it is important to understand that, in the case of Rutherford, the reason for this termination in production was not, as Thomas Hardy suggests it was for him, disgust at the 'howling'[27] reviews and at the public's refusal to appreciate the 'morality'[28] of his last novels. For Mark Rutherford, *Clara Hopgood* was not simply the last novel, it was the culmination of a process of thought that had been evolving ever since his first book was written. Mark Rutherford produced no other novel after *Clara Hopgood* because he had written all that he had to do in this form. His silence was the mark of completion.

Clara Hopgood is the most explicitly intellectual of the novels. Not only are its characters the most eloquent but there is the sense of their expressing unique dilemmas rather than, as was often the case for characters in the earlier works, embodying representative difficulties. The story is slight but strange. Madge and Clara Hopgood are well-educated sisters. Madge falls in love, is engaged and becomes pregnant, only to realize that she doesn't care for the man. He proposes, more than once, but she chooses to bring up her child alone. Because of Madge's pregnancy the family are forced to move to London, even though Clara dislikes the city and her mother fears the expense of living there. Shortly after their arrival in London, Mrs Hopgood dies and Clara is obliged to find work in order to support her sister and the expected child. Clara meets and is loved by a widower, loves him in return, but deliberately gives him up to her sister, and herself goes off to Italy to join Mazzini's struggle for a united Italy. This slightness is entirely intentional. As always for Rutherford, the interplay of ideas and character is more important than story. This final novel is the one most substantially grounded in ideas; and yet in spite of its concern for ideas, the book is not dogmatic. Though intelligent conversation composes most of the novel, the wisdom that the characters embody is not easily translatable into anecdote, so that the responsibility of moral judgement is placed firmly upon the reader.

At the heart of *Clara Hopgood* is a love story. There is no shortage of love stories in Rutherford's novels, but often love in his work becomes subject to a kind of inertia, or it is a means to personal discovery and not an end in itself. In *Clara Hopgood* love is the dynamic of the characters, the impetus for both the narrative and intellectual movement of the novel. And yet, in spite of the fact that the novel develops out of an act of lovemaking, Rutherford is only superficially interested in sexual love and then only as a means by which the characters become more conscious of themselves and of the limitation and complexity of reason and impulse. In *Catharine Furze*, the novel that precedes *Clara Hopgood*, Rutherford asks 'what is love?', his reply is that 'There is no such thing: there are loves, and they are all different'.[29] In this final novel the idea of love in its widest sense is explored. The novel presents many different kinds of love: that of a mother for her daughter, the love between sisters, sexual love, the love that proceeds from duty, Baruch's love of thought. Above all, it is the analysis of the love that goes beyond the personal that is at the centre of the narrative.

In *Clara Hopgood* love is seen consistently from the woman's point of view. Frank Palmer, though a good man, scarcely has a mind of his own and, though Baruch Cohen is given a full and complex character, it is still Clara's response that matters most. Mrs Marshall's loveless relationship, lacking the distraction of a child to disguise her husband's indifference, shows the failure of marriage as a female vocation. Through its exploration of love *Clara Hopgood* addresses quietly what was coming to be thought of as the 'Woman Question'. This 'question', whilst it remains central to the novel and is treated with genuine commitment and seriousness, is not commented on by the narrator explicitly. As always, judgement is left with the reader. This is because Rutherford is more concerned with recognizing and understanding human need than making a political statement. Rutherford presents Madge and Clara as educated women, whose schooling fits them to conduct a discussion that touches upon ideas of 'true law', human nature, 'principle', instinct, reason, right and wrong,[30] and yet they do so within a debate that takes as its starting point the importance and desirability of romantic love and the inevitability of marriage for women.

When we first encounter them, Madge and Clara are playing chess, a notoriously 'male' game. Madge is losing and Clara attributes her sister's lack of success to a failure in 'planning and . . . forecasting'.[31] Whilst Madge concedes that such calculation is a definite advantage when playing a game, she insists that in life and, more importantly, in the selection of a husband, her preference of instinct will tell. Underpinning this discussion of the relative merits of impulse and calculation is an almost Lawrencian assumption that every woman is entitled to experience the transformation that love can bring.

Madge's wish that someone will make love to Clara is not primarily romantic. For her, love is 'the one emotion common to the whole world', the experience that most 'reveals character'.[32] In a note in one of his journals, Hale White writes of love precisely as Madge might have done if she had alluded to Spinoza:

> When we really love we cannot believe that our love is mortal. We feel, not only that it is immortal, but that it is eternal, in the sense in which Spinoza uses the word. It is not the attraction of something entirely limited and personal to that which is also limited and personal.[33]

Love, in *Clara Hopgood*, is the means then to a Spinozan unity of the finite and the infinite, a way of progressing beyond what is 'entirely limited and personal'. It is important that this is remembered if Clara's action at the close of the novel is to be appreciated as something more than self-sacrifice. Her acceptance of a destiny beyond the personal is the fulfilment of the novel's intellectual action.

What crushes Madge when she realises the implications that

her pregnancy will have for her mother and sister is not shame or remorse, things so 'limited and personal' as to be of no real consequence according to Spinoza, but the 'sense of cruel injustice to those who loved her'.[34] Rutherford tells us that, had she believed in the 'common creed'[35] (the creed that feeds Mark Rutherford's discontent in the *Autobiography* and which in *The Early Life* had concentrated Hale White's thoughts upon his own salvation), Madge might have been tempted to overlook the 'injustice' to her mother and Clara. But the difference in this novel is that Madge's impulse to flee to the country and be alone does not come, as had Rutherford's and Hale White's discovery of Nature, from a need to escape the claustrophobic sense of self that Calvinism had imposed upon them. Here, religion is not an issue. The pressure that drives Madge away from London is intellectual and not theological.

In the porch of the country church, 'sick and despairing', Madge 'could not help being touched' by the quiet stillness of the scenery around her:

> she thought to herself how strange the world is – so transcendent both in glory and in horror; a world capable of such scenes as those before her, and a world in which such suffering as hers could be; a world infinite both ways.[36]

Madge's situation and her setting recalls many scenes in Hardy's novels. However, it is in the spirit behind Rutherford's passage that his distinction from Hardy emerges. In Hardy the mill-pond that Madge gazes into would have issued an invitation to suicide. Hardy's emphasis would have fallen upon the 'inner' deadness of Madge's feelings rather than upon the 'peculiar' beauty of the 'living' scene. The power of place and nature is an active force in Rutherford but in a different manner to Hardy. In Rutherford's fiction nature is not indifferent to human suffering, rather it functions as a beneficent force, recalling the Wordsworth's lines that were so important to Hale White:

> Nature never did betray
> The heart that loved her.

The scene around Madge deprives her for an instant of all ability to dwell on her own sorrows – just long enough to prevent her from resisting its beauty. She is rendered momentarily unconscious of her self so as to be made conscious of the idea of that self as part of some larger order. It is an order capable of generating terrible extremes it is true, though even in that, for Rutherford, preferable to Hardy's vision of random indifference.

Hale White writes that Spinoza frees us from sorrow by thinking. Madge's contemplation of her part within the scene around her, though it provides no explanation as to why she should suffer, does impress upon her a sense of the futility of complaint. Her composure is not fatalism, however, but rather the apprehension that there is an organization, even if her mind cannot fully comprehend it, in the corresponding 'glory' and 'horror' of the universe.

Madge's implicit apprehension of the Spinozan unity of the finite and infinite is emotional and sensual: the serenity of the churchyard, the beauty of the scene and the sublimity of the 'Kyrie' combine to inspire her to share in their composure. Through Baruch Cohen, who shares the philosopher's forename and occupation,[37] Spinoza's ideas are stated directly:

> Perhaps the highest of all truths is incapable of demonstration and can only be stated . . . I believe that inability to imagine a thing is not a reason for its non-existence. If the infinite is forced upon me, the fact that I cannot picture it does not disprove it. I believe, also, in thought and the soul, and it is nothing to me that I cannot explain them by attributes belonging to the body . . . I believe that all thought is a manifestation of the Being, who is One, whom you may call God if you like, and that, as It was never created, It will never be destroyed.[38]

What Baruch presents here is Spinoza's 'adequate idea'. His philosophy, like Spinoza's, has its foundation in a mathematical training which demands the acceptance of 'ideas which are inconsistent with the notion that the imagination is a measure of all things'. Though he admits to having no 'theory which explains the universe', Baruch can be content in what he does know: 'It is something', he insists, 'to know that the sky is as real as the earth'.[39] If what is beyond physical and mental comprehension is no less real than the ground we stand on, why make the mind the measure of all that can be known, Baruch suggests. The 'modification' of religious belief that reading Wordsworth's *Lyrical Ballads* comprises in the *Autobiography* and *The Early Life* is mediated in *Clara Hopgood* by Baruch Cohen. Cohen's apprehension of the 'One in the Many'[40] takes us beyond the anxiety of personal destiny and a Christian frame of thought towards a cultural and spiritual inclusiveness.

The characters of *Clara Hopgood* are highly self-conscious beings, and yet Rutherford shows how their knowledge is incomplete. Again and again they fail fully to comprehend the complexity of their own motivation. When Madge first meets Frank Palmer she sees in him the perfect partner. She has 'read something of passion', we are told, but it is not until she encounters Frank that she discovers 'what the white intensity of [passion's] flame in a man could be'.[41] Madge's intellectual apprehension of 'passion', gained chiefly from books, is unrealised until she becomes involved with Frank. One consequence of her reading and education is that Madge feels the need to know (passion) from the inside as well as from without. Used to testing her ideas and eager for experience, Madge 'experiments' with Frank. Her exhilaration comes as much from her power to control and manipulate desire as from passion itself. As Frank embraces her:

> She released herself a trifle, held her head back as if she desired to survey him apart from her, so that the ecstasy of union might be renewed, and then fell on his neck.[42]

Curiosity and physical responsiveness are equally matched here. For all her maturity and intelligence, at this moment Madge is like a clever child, bright enough to want to discover, but too unworldly to realize the dangers of playing with 'ecstasy'. The union that she imagines is really no union at all, since beyond their excitement there is nothing shared between the lovers: '*her* emotion enveloped *her*' (my emphases); Frank is 'beside himself'.[43] What is remarkable in this is that Madge's sexual curiosity attracts no censure from Rutherford. Later, when she and Frank take shelter from the storm, the narrative does not record their lovemaking. Rutherford is far more concerned with the circumstances and disguised motivations under which Madge and Frank become so intimate than he is with the act itself, either as a literary event or as conduct to be condemned.

In *Frank Palmer* Madge's belief that love reveals character is confirmed, though not in the manner she might have hoped. Anxious to prevent herself from having to admit her disappointment at his failure to match her intellectually, Madge tries to imagine hidden depths in Frank. But Rutherford makes it clear that all there is of him is visible from the surface. Though he is 'hearty', 'affectionate' and 'so cheerful that it was impossible not to love him',[44] Frank lacks any kind of substance. In spite of being surrounded at home by 'every influence which was pure and noble',[45] he remains unreflective.[46] Precisely because he is weak in this way, Frank wants desperately to act honourably towards Madge after they have made love; but, because his honour is compounded with weakness, it is for the wrong reasons. Frank's protestations to Madge are blunted by a preoccupation with the trouble he is in. His offer to wed Madge comes less from a sense of marriage as the complement of love than from the fear that under the circumstances it is the only thing they can do. Frank has no sense of the mistake he makes in repeatedly pleading for forgiveness where he ought to be protesting unqualified love. Nevertheless, in spite of his intellectual weakness, Frank's genuine distress for Madge makes clear that he is no brute and the novel attempts no judgement of him. Compared with Frank's fearful acquiescence to convention, Madge's absolute refusal to do the 'right' thing seems an act of principle and personal integrity, though Rutherford is uncompromising in his insistence upon the terrible consequences that her integrity holds for her mother and sister.

Clara Hopgood is a precisely structured, almost schematic novel. The first half concerns itself predominantly with Madge's story. The second half is given over to Clara's narrative, her brief involvement with Baruch Cohen, her 'sacrifice' and eventual exit from the novel. Compared with the 'drama' of Madge's opening, Clara's story emerges as relatively insubstantial. One contemporary reviewer complained that Clara, 'who is presumably meant to be the heroine, is not adequately expounded';[47] another, that the story only touches on Clara 'indirectly', so that the reader might 'wonder whether the title is not a misnomer';[48] yet another asserts that 'the story of 'Clara Hopgood' is chiefly about her sister Madge'.[49] The inability of these reviewers to understand why the novel is named after Clara comes from a failure to see how the expected continuities of the narrative are broken in order to put idea, discussion and reflection into the foreground. The difference between the sisters' stories and the manner in which they are presented to the reader is fundamental to the novel both as argument and exploration. Madge's struggle has been easier to read because it is largely explicable from the 'outside', it has been one with the flesh. Clara's 'action' will be almost entirely undisclosed, her emotions displaced into the descriptions of nature that occur more frequently in the second part of the novel.

Rutherford's novels always tend to have a structure rather than plot.[50] Madge and Clara are made to seem at the start of the novel like poles in a debate: one speaking for impulse, the other for reason. Yet as the narrative unfolds we are forced to recognize that they are much closer, that they partake of each other's nature to an extent that their expressed philosophies would appear to deny. The second half of the novel reintroduces their differences along a more complex route than the opposition of reason and feeling.

All the chief characters of *Clara Hopgood* depend to some extent for their definition upon their counterparts in the 'opposing' half of the book. Thus Baruch Cohen, a profoundly educated, thoughtful man, led by religious enquiries, emerges once Frank has played his part as his antithesis. Mrs Caffyn's flexibility and understanding, very much the result of practical experience of life with all its inherent contradictions, contrasts generally with the Hopgood tradition of learning and profound thought on agreed issues. More than anything, Mrs Caffyn represents a personal religion, a natural sense of piety that is no respecter of persons. In contrast to the sisters, Mrs Caffyn is a remarkably free character whose estimate of 'the relative values of the virtues and of the relative sinfulness of sins was original'.[51] Her wisdom is practical, acquired through experience of life and not as the result of the liberal education that Madge and Clara have received.

The 'love' that Madge and Frank feel for each other is founded in passion. Though the climax of this love comes suddenly, its narrative growth allows time for Rutherford to tell how they meet and become intimate, so that their lovemaking comes less as a shock than as confirmation of our expectations. The manner in which Baruch Cohen and Clara fall in love is scarcely recognizable by comparison. The difference will not depend upon the presentation of a 'moral' love, a happy ending, to balance the earlier 'immoral' unsatisfactory one; the balance that Rutherford seeks works less by this kind of contrast than by debate and exploration.

The relationship between Clara and Baruch, even whilst it is clearly much more profound than friendship, is impossible to comprehend in the purely 'romantic' terms that the precedent of Frank and Madge invites. Part of the difficulty in comprehending the love that develops between Clara and Baruch has to do with the way in which Rutherford deliberately accelerates the pace of their intimacy, and part with the actual character of that intimacy. Without the expected romantic preliminaries, this second love affair is fully fledged before the reader has time to anticipate and so realise its occurrence. Where previously we were able to guess the way that Madge and Frank's story might develop, we are forced to struggle just to keep track with Clara and Baruch. Like the lovers themselves, readers are surprised by the way in which the apparently casual becomes serious. Baruch and Clara become intimate too soon, they talk too confidentially for the reader confidently to follow their conversations; and if we are not put off by the sophistication of their discussion, we are mystified by their ability to discover intuitively its implicit meaning and course.[52]

This second love is an intellectual one, consummated not primarily in physical attraction but in mutual self-disclosure. Because they are so self-reflective their love is bound to reveal itself in intellectual sympathy rather than physical compulsion. At the beginning of the novel Madge voices her fear that, confronted by a lover, Clara might 'hold off for six months and consider, and consider, and ask [herself] whether he had such virtues and whether he could make [her] happy?'[53] In the event, it is Baruch and not Clara who hesitates, fearful that he might be in love with his own idea of a woman, rather than with Clara herself. Though they have seemed so similar, it is in her freedom from this kind of fearful questioning that Clara differs from Baruch. Clara is subject to no such testing rationalism as he is. She realises that the kind of logical completeness that he looks for is not applicable to love; her certainty about him is founded not upon rational but emotional security. While Baruch agonises over the distinction between idea and emotion, Clara sees their situation with a clarity that is grounded in the most simple and direct deductions: here is a man 'whom she could love'.[54] Nor is Rutherford coy in allowing Clara's assent to encompass the more mundane aspects of love:

> She thought, too – why should she not think of it? – of the future, of the release from her dreary occupation, of a happy home with independence, and she thought of the children that might be.[55]

Even though marriage to a man who could not 'give her all her intellect demanded'[56] would be impossible for Clara, Rutherford will not deny – 'why should she not think of it?' – the importance of the more ordinary benefits that marrying Baruch would mean to a woman in Clara's position:

> A husband was to be had for a look, for a touch . . . A little house rose before her eyes . . . there was a bright fire on the hearth, and there were children round it; without the look, the touch, there

would be solitude, silence and a childless old age, so much more
to be feared by a woman than a man.[57]

Clara realises what is at stake here, not just for the moment but
for her whole future. The idea of 'solitude, silence and a childless
old age' holds much to be rationally feared. Rutherford is answer-
ing the radical feminist criticism of the home and childbearing as
instruments of female oppression by insisting upon their apprehension in individual and practical rather than political terms.
Clara's view of what Baruch's love means is not simply or naively
'romantic'; it takes into account the 'demands' of her intellect,
emotional fulfilment, physical comfort, personal security, bio-
logical compulsion. The inclusiveness of Clara's sense of what
Baruch's love would mean to her life gives to her eventual
determination to disclaim it the character of renunciation.

Rutherford has presented all manner of flawed relationships
in his novels. Here, where love is absolutely genuine, for Clara
its expression has to be achieved through something more than
the personal – love takes on a larger aspect. Baruch is worthy of
Clara but ultimately the novel is less concerned with him for
whom the lighter destiny of personal love is sufficient.

Clara Hopgood is a novel of difficult explanations that
Rutherford quite deliberately leaves only half executed: why
Madge must reject Frank; why Clara must give up Baruch.
Moreover, explanations, when they are offered, are given
obliquely and come from unexpected quarters, as with Madge's
reconcilement in the country churchyard. After Clara realizes
that she must refuse Baruch there is no further explicit exposition of her actions. The scene leaves the reader more perplexed
even than Baruch who could not be sure, as we are, of Clara's
love for him. Only much later, as Clara at the start of the
group's country holiday watches two figures in the distance, do
we receive some inkling of the motivation for her refusal to
answer Baruch:

It was impossible to mistake them; they were Madge and Baruch . . .'
The message then was authentic,' she [Clara] said to herself. 'I
thought I could not have misunderstood it.'[58]

Here, conclusively, we are able to realize Clara's refusal of Baruch as something more profound than the inevitable, if sincere, outcome of a personality predisposed always to see too many reasons to be able to surrender to compulsion. The idea that Baruch and Madge could love each other had come like a revelation to Clara earlier, seeing them together here is the fulfilment of that prophesy.

Clara's renunciation of Baruch has a more profound heroism about it than appears at first. Giving Baruch up to her sister means more than the forfeiture of a secure future; she must realize how she deprives herself of discovering any substantial purpose in life. Her relationship with Madge and her child has been, up to this point, that discharged by a husband and father; Clara works to support the family. In emotional terms the prospect of the necessary break with Madge and her child is like a bereavement for Clara. Looking forward, the prospect is bleak. And yet it is through this bleakness, in which it is difficult not to recall Madge's nadir in the country churchyard (and beyond that the despair of Rutherford and Hale White), that enlightenment comes.

Earlier, Madge had been compelled to accept that the awful 'strangeness' of the world lay less in its apparent toleration of human suffering than in the idea that it was 'transcendent both in glory and horror'. The organization of the narrative of *Clara Hopgood*, so full of reflections and symmetries, obliges us, in thinking of Clara, to remember Madge, and so to consider that this is 'a world infinite both ways'. We know that Clara had thought fondly of herself as a wife and a mother, but, put to the test, hers is revealed as an abstract passion, a yearning not for self-satisfaction but for justice in the terms that Mazzini describes:

'Whenever any real good is done it is by a crusade; that is to say, the cross must be raised and appeal be made to something *above* the people. No system based on rights will stand. Never will society be permanent till it is founded on duty. If we consider our rights exclusively, we extend them over the rights of our neighbours. If the oppressed classes had the power to obtain their rights tomorrow, and with the rights came no deeper sense of duty, the new order, for the simple reason that the oppressed are no better than their oppressors, would be just as unstable as that which preceded it.'[59]

It is Clara's 'duty' to bring together Madge and Baruch because they need each other, regardless of her own claims or 'rights'. In submitting to this Clara reveals a Spinozan sense of the forces behind individual life. She needs something above and beyond the personal for the expression of her love. Nor is her refusal of Baruch what could be called a sacrifice. Rather, there is in her the apprehension of the 'real good', a true delight in her own perception of a 'law' that, in superseding the personal, is 'stable' and 'permanent'. Her decision is consolidated by a wider sense of her own purpose and that of the universe:

Clara, always a light sleeper, woke between three and four, rose and went to the little casement window which had been left open all night. Below her, on the left, the church was just discernible, and on the right, the broad chalk uplands leaned to the south, and were waving with green barley and wheat. Underneath her lay the cottage garden, with its rows of beehives in the north-east corner, sheltered from the cold winds by the thick hedge. It had evidently been raining a little, for the drops hung on the currant bushes, but the clouds had been driven by the south westerly wind into the eastern sky, where they lay in a long, low grey band. Not a sound was to be heard, save every now and then the crow of a cock or the short cry of a just-awakened thrush. High up on the zenith, the approach of the sun to the horizon was proclaimed by the most delicate tints of rose-colour, but the cloud bank above him was dark and untouched, although the blue which was over it, was every moment becoming paler. Clara watched; she was moved even to tears by the beauty of the scene, but she was stirred by something more than beauty, just as he who was in the Spirit and beheld a throne and One sitting thereon, saw something more than loveliness, although He was radiant with the colour of jasper and there was a rainbow round about Him like an emerald to look upon. In a few moments more the fire just at one point came blinding, in another second the sun emerged, the first arrowy shaft passed into her chamber, the first shadow was cast, and it was day. She put her hands to her face; the tears fell faster, but she wiped them away and her great purpose was fixed.[60]

From her position, rooted in humanity, between 'church' and 'broad chalk uplands', within a landscape whose face is marked with fields of 'barley and wheat', 'cottage garden' and 'beehives', by the human endeavour to make the earth sustain the body, Clara watches the working of the universe at large and the implicit continuity that underpins both life and death reveals itself before her, as if for her benefit alone. Rutherford describes the onset of the dawn in terms at once of burgeoning beauty and precise natural accuracy. The new day 'proclaims' an enlightenment for Clara that surpasses the magnificence of the dawn. What light there exists, and its delicacy, is felt more profoundly for the lingering darkness in the 'cloud-bank'. What moves Clara though is 'something more than the beauty' of the natural scene; it is what is for her implicit in its beauty: an order, a purpose. Though we do not yet know it, Clara has already made up her mind to work for Mazzini on a secret mission in Italy.

When, late in George Eliot's *Middlemarch*, Dorothea looks out from her window to the man with a bundle on his back and the woman carrying a baby, one has the sense that it is impossible for her to avoid seeing herself as a part of the world at large, even though she feels separate. What Dorothea sees is an image of how life might be carried on, even as a burden. Though she feels the 'largeness of the world', the lightening sky here is a backdrop for Dorothea, it is the human foreground that Eliot privileges. What is fixed for Clara by her vision at the end of Rutherford's novel, is not any sense of human community but rather a 'great purpose', a purpose that is alienating in imposing demands that might be considered beyond the bounds of human duty, the laying down of one's life for a principle. Rutherford wants to envisage in Clara a destiny for a woman's life even bigger than that which Eliot finds for Dorothea, a sense of mission like Saint Theresa's: supra-personal, a total dedication of the self. *Middlemarch*, published twenty-five years before Rutherford's final novel, comes to the conclusion that the time and the 'medium' (Penguin, p. 896) that might give rise to a Saint Theresa is past. *Clara Hopgood* challenges Eliot's conclusion; in Clara we are shown, not only what a 'modern' saint might look like, but how she might come into being. In Chapter 9 of Rutherford's first novel, *The Autobiography*, the character Theresa (a version of George Eliot herself, with whom WHW had worked as a young man), rejects Rutherford's wish that novelists 'would not write as if love were the very centre and sum of human existence'. Theresa insists that love 'is the subject of all subjects', and that 'it is the great fact of life' that 'keeps the world straight'. It is as if in *Clara Hopgood* the character of Clara implicitly answers Theresa by suggesting that if one was to love in such an exemplary manner, then only the whole of mankind would be sufficient as subject.

LORRAINE DAVIES

References

1. *The Early Life of Mark Rutherford (W. Hale White) by Himself*, (London: Humphrey Milford, 1913), p. 21. Hereafter cited as *Early Life*.

2. The Test Act (1673) made it illegal for any persons not receiving communion in the Church of England to hold office under the Crown and the Corporation Act (1661) did the same for offices in municipal corporations.

3. *Early Life*, pp. 59, 62.

4. *Early Life*, p 62.

5. William White, *To Think or not to Think*, pamphlet (Bedford: John G. Nall, 1852).

6. *Early Life*, pp. 71–2.

7. *The Autobiography of Mark Rutherford: Dissenting Minister*, edited by his friend, Reuben Shapcott (London: Trubner and Co., 1881) and *Mark Rutherford's Deliverance: Being the second part*

of his Autobiography, edited by his friend Rouben Shapcott (London: Trubner and Co., 1885).

8. E. A. Baker, 'Mark Rutherford and Others' in *The History of the English Novel*, 10 vols (London: Riverside Press, 1938) IX, 97–121 (p. 97).

9. Unpublished letter, the original of which is in the Shorter Correspondence, Brotherton Library, University of Leeds, 11190–07.

10. *Early Life*, p. 78.

11. Mark Rutherford, *The Revolution in Tanner's Lane*, edited by his friend Reuben Shapcott (London: Trubner and Co., 1887).

12. Mark Rutherford, *Miriam's Schooling and Other Papers*, edited by his friend Reuben Shapcott (London: Kegan Paul, Trench, Trubner and Co. Ltd., 1890).

13. Zachariah Coleman is the main character in *The Revolution in Tanner's Lane*.

14. Mark Rutherford, *Catharine Furze*, edited by his friend Reuben Shapcott (London: T. Fisher Unwin, 1893).

15. Rutherford's novels are, for their period, remarkably economic. They are anecdotal in character, unconcerned with settling the destinies of all the characters, and structured about ideas which give them an internal shape. Above all, they are intimate and personal in tone and relation with the reader.

16. Writing to a friend, Matthew Arnold urged him 'On no account ever to miss anything that Mark Rutherford ever wrote', Irvin Stock, *William Hale White (Mark Rutherford)* London: Unwin, 1956), p. 3.

17. William Dean Howells wrote of Rutherford's novels that they 'may yet mark a new era in fiction ... they carry so deep a sense of truthfulness to the reader, they are so far in temper from any sort of mere artistry, they are so simply and nobly serious.' Ibid.

18. Review of *Clara Hopgood* in the *Athenaeum*, 3590, 15 August 1896.

19. W. Robertson Nicholl writing as 'Claudius Clear' in the *British Weekly*, 9 July 1896.

20. Stock (1956), p. 197.

21. John Lucas, *The Literature of Change: Studies in the Nineteenth Century Provincial Novel* (New York: Barnes and Noble, 1977), p. 110.

22. David Daiches, *Some Late Victorian Attitudes* (London: André Deutsch, 1969), p. 123.

23. Thomas Hardy told the feminist Millicent Garrett Fawcett, 'we are educating them [Hardy's readership] by degrees', Rosemarie Morgan, *Women and Sexuality in the Novels of Thomas Hardy* (London: Routledge, 1988), p. 113.

24. Michael Millgate, *The Life and Work of Thomas Hardy* (London: Macmillan, 1989), p. 296.

25. Millgate (1989), p. 304.

26. *The Well-Beloved* was revised and reissued in 1997 but was first published serially in 1892.

27. Millgate (1989), p. 287.

28. Millgate (1989), p. 297.

29. *Catharine Furze*, Chapter 10.

30. *Clara Hopgood*, pp. 16–18.

31. ibid., p. 15.

32. ibid., p. 38.

33. Mark Rutherford, *More Pages from a Journal* (London: Henry Frowde, 1910), p. 234.

34. *Clara Hopgood*, p. 50.

35. ibid., p. 50.

36. ibid., p. 51.

37. See second note, p. 74.

38. *Clara Hopgood*, p. 126.

39. ibid., p. 126.

40. ibid., p. 99.

41. ibid., p. 41.

42. ibid., p. 37

43. ibid., p. 42.

44. ibid., p. 20.

45. ibid., p. 19.

46. ibid., p. 19.

47. Review of *Clara Hopgood* in the *Athenaeum*, 3590, 15 August 1896.

48. Review of *Clara Hopgood* in the *Academy*, 1267, 15 August 1896.

49. Review of *Clara Hopgood* in the *Critic*, 15 August 1896.

50. The bipartite structure of *Clara Hopgood* recalls the two parts of

the *Autobiography* which are completed by the *Deliverance*. *The Revolution in Tanner's Lane* comprises two halves connected by one character. In *Miriam's Schooling* there is a deliberate contrast between Miriam Tacchi and Michael Trevanion.

51. *Clara Hopgood*, p. 55.

52. This is especially so in the conversation that covers pp. 95–6. When Clara says 'Do you believe that the good does not necessarily survive?' we realise how, beneath the conversation that we have been able to follow as easily as the speakers until now, there has been another unspoken, more intimate dialogue. The break in explicit continuity that pulls the reader up short here goes unnoticed by Clara and Baruch. For them, no break exists. Baruch shows no surprise at what to the reader is a disjointed enquiry and is able immediately to lift his response from below the surface of the discussion, so to speak, completely unaware of any switch in 'levels'.

53. *Clara Hopgood*, p. 17.

54. ibid., p. 120.

55. ibid., p. 106.

56. ibid., p. 120.

57. ibid., p. 120.

58. ibid., p. 130.

59. ibid., p. 123.

60. ibid., p. 129.

NOTE ON THE TEXT

The text of *Clara Hopgood* used for this Everyman edition is the third impression (1907) of the 1896 T. Fisher Unwin edition.

CLARA HOPGOOD

were somewhat marred by an uneven nasal outline, but this was redeemed by the curved lips of a mouth which was small and rather compressed, and by a definite, symmetrical and graceful figure. Her eyes were grey, with a curious peculiarity in them. Ordinarily they were steady, strong eyes, excellent and renowned optical instruments. Over and over again she had detected, along the stretch of the Eastthorpe road, approaching visitors, and had named them when her companions could see nothing but specks. Occasionally, however, these steady, strong, grey eyes utterly changed. They were the same eyes, the same colour, but they ceased to be mere optical instruments and became instruments of expression, transmissive of radiance to such a degree that the light which was reflected from them seemed insufficient to account for it. It was also curious that this change, though it must have been accompanied by some emotion, was just as often not attended by any other sign of it. Clara was, in fact, little given to any display of feeling.

Madge, four years younger than her sister, was of a different type altogether, and one more easily comprehended. She had very heavy dark hair, and she had blue eyes, a combination which fascinated Fenmarket. Fenmarket admired Madge more than it was admired by her in return, and she kept herself very much to herself, notwithstanding what it considered to be its temptations. If she went shopping she nearly always went with her sister; she stood aloof from all the small gaieties of the town; walked swiftly through its streets, and repelled, frigidly and decisively, all offers, and they were not a few, which had been made to her by the sons of the Fenmarket tradesfolk. Fenmarket pronounced her 'stuck-up', and having thus labelled her, considered it had exhausted her. The very important question, Whether there was anything which naturally stuck up? Fenmarket never asked. It was a great relief to that provincial little town in 1844,* in this and in other cases, to find a word which released it from further mental effort and put out of sight any troublesome, straggling, indefinable qualities which it would otherwise have been forced to examine and name. Madge was certainly stuck-up, but the projection above those around her was not artificial. Both she and her sister found the ways of Fenmarket were not to their taste. The reason lay partly in their nature and partly in their history.

Mrs Hopgood was the widow of the late manager in the Fenmarket branch of the bank of Rumbold, Martin & Rumbold, and when her husband died she had of course to leave the Bank Buildings. As her income was somewhat straitened, she was obliged to take a small house, and she was now living next door to the Crown and Sceptre, the principal inn in the town. There was then no fringe of villas to Fenmarket for retired quality; the private houses and shops were all mixed together, and Mrs Hopgood's cottage was squeezed in between the ironmonger's and the inn. It was very much lower than either of its big neighbours, but it had a brass knocker and a bell, and distinctly asserted and maintained a kind of aristocratic superiority.

Mr Hopgood was not a Fenmarket man. He came straight from London to be manager. He was in the bank of the London agents of Rumbold, Martin & Rumbold, and had been strongly recommended by the city firm as just the person to take charge of a branch which needed thorough reorganisation. He succeeded, and nobody in Fenmarket was more respected. He lived, however, a life apart from his neighbours, excepting so far as business was concerned. He went to church once on Sunday because the bank expected him to go, but only once, and had nothing to do with any of its dependent institutions. He was a great botanist, very fond of walking, and in the evening, when Fenmarket generally gathered itself into groups for gossip, either in the street or in back parlours, or in the Crown and Sceptre, Mr Hopgood, tall, lean and stately, might be seen wandering along the solitary roads searching for flowers, which, in that part of the world, were rather scarce. He was also a great reader of the best books, English, German and French, and held high doctrine, very high for those days, on the training of girls, maintaining that they need, even more than boys, exact discipline and knowledge. Boys, he thought, find health in an occupation; but an uncultivated, unmarried girl dwells with her own untutored thoughts, which often breed disease. His two daughters, therefore, received an education much above that which was usual amongst people in their position, and each of them – an unheard of wonder in Fenmarket – had spent some time in a school in Weimar.* Mr Hopgood was also peculiar in his way of dealing with his children. He talked to them and made them talk to him, and whatever they read was translated into speech; thought, in his house, was vocal.

Mrs Hopgood, too, had been the intimate friend of her husband, and was the intimate friend of her daughters. She was now nearly sixty, but still erect and graceful, and everybody could see that the picture of a beautiful girl of one-and-twenty, which hung opposite the fireplace, had once been her portrait. She had been brought up, as thoroughly as a woman could be brought up, in those days, to be a governess. The war prevented her education abroad, but her father, who was a clergyman, not too rich, engaged a French emigrant lady to live in his house to teach her French and other accomplishments. She consequently spoke French perfectly, and she could also read and speak Spanish fairly well, for the French lady had spent some years in Spain. Mr Hopgood had never been particularly in earnest about religion, but his wife was a believer, neither High Church nor Low Church, but inclined towards a kind of quietism not uncommon in the Church of England, even during its bad time, a reaction against the formalism which generally prevailed. When she married, Mrs Hopgood did not altogether follow her husband. She never separated herself from her faith, and never would have confessed that she had separated herself from her church. But although she knew that his creed externally was not hers, her own was not sharply cut, and she persuaded herself that, in substance, his and her belief were identical. As she grew older her relationship to the Unseen became more and more intimate, but she was less and less inclined to criticise her husband's freedom, or to impose on the children a rule which they would certainly have observed, but only for her sake. Every now and then she felt a little lonely; when, for example, she read one or two books which were particularly her own; when she thought of her dead father and mother, and when she prayed her solitary prayer. Mr Hopgood took great pains never to disturb that sacred moment. Indeed, he never for an instant permitted a finger to be laid upon what she considered precious. He loved her because she had the strength to be what she was when he first knew her and she had so fascinated him. He would have been disappointed if the mistress of his youth had become some other person, although the change, in a sense, might have been development and progress. He did really love her piety, too, for its own sake. It mixed something with her behaviour to him and to the children which charmed him, and he did not know from what other existing source anything comparable to it could be supplied. Mrs Hopgood seldom went to church. The church, to be sure, was horribly dead, but she did not give that as a reason. She had, she said, an infirmity, a strange restlessness which prevented her from sitting still for an hour. She often pleaded this excuse, and her husband and daughters never, by word or smile, gave her the least reason to suppose that they did not believe her.

CHAPTER 2

Both Clara and Madge went first to an English day-school, and Clara went straight from this school to Germany, but Madge's course was a little different. She was not very well, and it was decided that she should have at least a twelvemonth in a boarding-school at Brighton before going abroad. It had been very highly recommended, but the head-mistress was Low Church and aggressive. Mr Hopgood, far away from the High and Low Church controversy,* came to the conclusion that, in Madge's case, the theology would have no effect on her. It was quite impossible, moreover, to find a school which would be just what he could wish it to be. Madge, accordingly, was sent to Brighton, and was introduced into a new world. She was just beginning to ask herself *why* certain things were right and other

things were wrong, and the Brighton answer was that the former
were directed by revelation and the latter forbidden, and that
the 'body' was an affliction to the soul, a means of 'probation',
our principal duty being to 'war' against it.

Madge's bedroom companion was a Miss Selina Fish, daughter of Barnabas Fish, Esquire, of Clapham, and merchant of the
City of London. Miss Fish was not traitorous at heart, but when
she found out that Madge had not been christened, she was so
overcome that she was obliged to tell her mother. Miss Fish was
really unhappy, and one cold night, when Madge crept into her
neighbour's bed, contrary to law, but in accordance with custom
when the weather was very bitter, poor Miss Fish shrank from
her, half-believing that something dreadful might happen if she
should by any chance touch unbaptised, naked flesh. Mrs Fish
told her daughter that perhaps Miss Hopgood might be a
Dissenter, and that although Dissenters were to be pitied, and
even to be condemned, many of them were undoubtedly among
the redeemed, as for example, that man of God, Dr Doddridge*
whose *Family Expositor* was read systematically at home, as
Selina knew. Then there were Matthew Henry* whose commentary her father preferred to any other, and the venerable saint,
the Reverend William Jay of Bath,* whom she was proud to call
her friend. Miss Fish, therefore, made further inquiries gently
and delicately, but she found to her horror that Madge had
neither been sprinkled nor immersed! Perhaps she was a Jewess
or a heathen! This was a happy thought, for then she might be
converted. Selina knew what interest her mother took in
missions to heathens and Jews; and if Madge, by the humble
instrumentality of a child, could be brought to the foot of the
Cross, what would her mother and father say? What would they
not say? Fancy taking Madge to Clapham in a nice white dress
– it should be white, thought Selina – and presenting her as a
saved lamb!

The very next night she began, –

'I suppose your father is a foreigner?'

'No, he is an Englishman.'

'But if he is an Englishman you must have been baptised, or

sprinkled, or immersed, and your father and mother must belong to church or chapel. I know there are thousands of wicked people who belong to neither, but they are drunkards and liars and robbers, and even they have their children christened.'

'Well, he is an Englishman,' said Madge, smiling.

'Perhaps,' said Selina, timidly, 'he may be – he may be – Jewish. Mamma and papa pray for the Jews every morning. They are not like other unbelievers.'

'No, he is certainly not a Jew.'

'What is he, then?'

'He is my papa and a very honest, good man.'

'Oh, my dear Madge! honesty is a broken reed. I have heard mamma say that she is more hopeful of thieves than honest people who think they are saved by works, for the thief who was crucified went to heaven, and if he had been only an honest man he never would have found the Saviour and would have gone to hell. Your father must be something.'

'I can only tell you again that he is honest and good.'

Selina was confounded. She had heard of those people who were *nothing*, and had always considered them as so dreadful that she could not bear to think of them. The efforts of her father and mother did not extend to them; they were beyond the reach of the preacher – mere vessels of wrath.* If Madge had confessed herself Roman Catholic, or idolator, Selina knew how to begin. She would have pointed out to the Catholic how unscriptural it was to suppose that anybody could forgive sins excepting God, and she would at once have been able to bring the idolator to his knees by exposing the absurdity of worshipping bits of wood and stone; but with a person who was nothing she could not tell what to do. She was puzzled to understand what right Madge had to her name. Who had any authority to say she was to be called Madge Hopgood? She determined at last to pray to God and again ask her mother's help.

She did pray earnestly that very night, and had not finished until long after Madge had said her Lord's Prayer. This was always said night and morning, both by Madge and Clara. They had been taught it by their mother. It was, by the way, one of poor Selina's troubles that Madge said nothing but the Lord's Prayer when she lay down and when she rose; of course, the Lord's Prayer was the best – how could it be otherwise, seeing that our Lord used it? – but those who supplemented it with no petitions of their own were set down as formalists, and it was always suspected that they had not received the true enlightenment from above. Selina cried to God till the counterpane was wet with her tears, but it was the answer from her mother which came first, telling her that however praiseworthy her intentions might be, argument with such a *dangerous* infidel as Madge would be most perilous, and she was to desist from it at once. Mrs Fish had by that post written to Miss Pratt, the schoolmistress, and Selina no doubt would not be exposed to further temptation. Mrs Fish's letter to Miss Pratt was very strong, and did not mince matters. She informed Miss Pratt that a wolf was in her fold, and that if the creature were not promptly expelled, Selina must be removed into safety. Miss Pratt was astonished, and instantly, as her custom was, sought the advice of her sister, Miss Hannah Pratt, who had charge of the wardrobes and household matters generally. Miss Hannah Pratt was never in the best of tempers, and just now was a little worse than usual. It was one of the rules of the school that no tradesmen's daughters should be admitted, but it was very difficult to draw the line, and when drawn, the Misses Pratt were obliged to admit it was rather ridiculous. There was much debate over an application by an auctioneer. He was clearly not a tradesman, but he sold chairs, tables and pigs, and, as Miss Hannah said, used vulgar language in recommending them. However, his wife had money; they lived in a pleasant house in Lewes, and the line went outside him. But when a druggist, with a shop in Bond Street, proposed his daughter, Miss Hannah took a firm stand. What is the use of a principle, she inquired severely, if we do not adhere to it? On the other hand, the druggist's daughter was the eldest of six, who might all come when they were old enough to leave home, and Miss Pratt thought there was a real difference between a druggist and, say, a bootmaker.

'Bootmaker!' said Miss Hannah with great scorn. 'I am

surprised that you venture to hint the remotest possibility of such a contingency.'

At last it was settled that the line should also be drawn outside the druggist. Miss Hannah, however, had her revenge. A tanner in Bermondsey with a house in Bedford Square, had sent two of his children to Miss Pratt's seminary. Their mother found out that they had struck up a friendship with a young person whose father compounded prescriptions for her, and when she next visited Brighton she called on Miss Pratt, reminded her that it was understood that her pupils would 'all be taken from a superior class in society', and gently hinted that she could not allow Bedford Square to be contaminated by Bond Street. Miss Pratt was most apologetic, enlarged upon the druggist's respectability, and more particularly upon his well-known piety and upon his generous contributions to the cause of religion. This, indeed, was what decided her to make an exception in his favour, and the piety also of his daughter was 'most exemplary'. However, the tanner's lady, although a shining light in the church herself, was not satisfied that a retail saint could produce a proper companion for her own offspring, and went away leaving Miss Pratt very uncomfortable.

'I warned you,' said Miss Hannah; 'I told you what would happen, and as to Mr Hopgood, I suspected him from the first. Besides, he is only a banker's clerk.'

'Well, what is to be done?'

'Put your foot down at once.' Miss Hannah suited the action to the word, and put down, with emphasis, on the hearthrug a very large, plate-shaped foot cased in a black felt shoe.

'But I cannot dismiss them. Don't you think it will be better, first of all, to talk to Miss Hopgood? Perhaps we could do her some good.'

'Good! Now, do you think we can do any good to an atheist? Besides, we have to consider our reputation. Whatever good we might do, it would be believed that the infection remained.'

'We have no excuse for dismissing the other.'

'Excuse! none is needed, nor would any be justifiable. Excuses are immoral. Say at once – of course politely and with regret –

that the school is established on a certain basis. It will be an
advantage to us if it is known why these girls do not remain. I
will dictate the letter, if you like.'

Miss Hannah Pratt had not received the education which had
been given to her younger sister, and therefore, was nominally
subordinate, but really she was chief. She considered it especially
her duty not only to look after the children's clothes, the servants
and the accounts, but to maintain *tone* everywhere in the
establishment, and to stiffen her sister when necessary, and
preserve in proper sharpness her orthodoxy, both in theology
and morals.

Accordingly, both the girls left, and both knew the reason for
leaving. The druggist's faith was sorely tried. If Miss Pratt's had
been a worldly seminary he would have thought nothing of such
behaviour, but he did not expect it from one of the faithful. The
next Sunday morning after he received the news, he stayed at
home out of his turn to make up any medicines which might be
urgently required, and sent his assistant to church.

As to Madge, she enjoyed her expulsion as a great joke, and
her Brighton experiences were the cause of much laughter. She
had learned a good deal while she was away from home, not
precisely what it was intended she should learn, and she came
back with a strong, insurgent tendency, which was even more
noticeable when she returned from Germany. Neither of the
sisters lived at the school in Weimar, but at the house of a lady
who had been recommended to Mrs Hopgood, and by this lady
they were introduced to the great German classics. She herself
was an enthusiast for Goethe, whom she well remembered in his
old age, and Clara and Madge, each of them in turn, learned to
know the poet as they would never have known him in England.
Even the town taught them much about him, for in many ways
it was expressive of him and seemed as if it had shaped itself for
him. It was a delightful time for them. They enjoyed the society
and constant mental stimulus; they loved the beautiful park; not
a separate enclosure walled round like an English park, but
suffering the streets to end in it, and in summer time there were
excursions into the Thüringer Wald,* generally to some point

memorable in history, or for some literary association. The drawback was the contrast, when they went home, with Fenmarket, with its dulness and its complete isolation from the intellectual world. At Weimar, in the evening, they could see Egmont* or hear Fidelio,* or talk with friends about the last utterance upon the Leben Jesu;* but the Fenmarket Egmont was a travelling wax-work show, its Fidelio psalm tunes, or at best some of Bishop's glees, performed by a few of the tradesfolk, who had never had an hour's instruction in music; and for theological criticism there were the parish church and Ram Lane Chapel. They did their best; they read their old favourites and subscribed for a German as well as an English literary weekly newspaper, but at times they were almost beaten. Madge more than Clara was liable to depression.

No Fenmarket maiden, other than the Hopgoods, was supposed to have any connection whatever, or to have any capacity for any connection with anything outside the world in which 'young ladies' dwelt, and if a Fenmarket girl read a book, a rare occurrence, for there were no circulating libraries there in those days, she never permitted herself to say anything more than that it was 'nice', or it was 'not nice', or she 'liked it' or did 'not like it'; and if she had ventured to say more, Fenmarket would have thought her odd, not to say a little improper. The Hopgood young women were almost entirely isolated, for the tradesfolk felt themselves uncomfortable and inferior in every way in their presence, and they were ineligible for rectory and brewery society, not only because their father was merely a manager, but because of their strange ways. Mrs Tubbs, the brewer's wife, thought they were due to Germany. From what she knew of Germany she considered it most injudicious, and even morally wrong, to send girls there. She once made the acquaintance of a German lady at an hotel at Tunbridge Wells, and was quite shocked. She could see quite plainly that the standard of female delicacy must be much lower in that country than in England. Mr Tubbs was sure Mrs Hopgood must have been French, and said to his daughters, mysteriously, 'you never can tell who Frenchwomen are'.

'But, papa,' said Miss Tubbs, 'you know Mrs Hopgood's maiden name; we found that out. It was Molyneux.'

'Of course, my dear, of course; but if she was a Frenchwoman resident in England she would prefer to assume an English name, that is to say if she wished to be married.'

Occasionally the Miss Hopgoods were encountered, and they confounded Fenmarket sorely. On one memorable occasion there was a party at the Rectory: it was the annual party into which were swept all the unclassifiable odds-and-ends which could not be put into the two gatherings which included the aristocracy and the democracy of the place. Miss Clara Hopgood amazed everybody by 'beginning talk', by asking Mrs Greatorex, her hostess, who had been far away to Sidmouth for a holiday, whether she had been to the place where Coleridge was born, and when the parson's wife said she had not, and that she could not be expected to make a pilgrimage to the birthplace of an infidel, Miss Hopgood expressed her surprise, and declared she would walk twenty miles any day to see Ottery St Mary.* Still worse, when somebody observed that an Anti-Corn-Law* lecturer was coming to Fenmarket, and the parson's daughter cried 'How horrid!' Miss Hopgood talked again, and actually told the parson that, so far as she had read upon the subject – fancy her reading about the Corn-Laws – the argument was all one way, and that after Colonel Thompson* nothing new could really be urged.

'What is so – ' she was about to say 'objectionable', but she recollected her official position and that she was bound to be politic – 'so odd and unusual', observed Mrs Greatorex to Mrs Tubbs afterwards, 'is not that Miss Hopgood should have radical views. Mrs Barker, I know, is a radical like her husband, but then she never puts herself forward, nor makes speeches. I never saw anything quite like it, except once in London at a dinner-party. Lady Montgomery then went on in much the same way, but she was a baronet's wife; the baronet was in Parliament; she received a good deal and was obliged to entertain her guests.'

Poor Clara! she was really very unobtrusive and very modest, but there had been constant sympathy between her and her father, not the dumb sympathy as between man and dog, but that which can manifest itself in human fashion.

CHAPTER 3

Clara and her father were both chess-players, and at the time at which our history begins, Clara had been teaching Madge the game for about six months.

'Check!' said Clara.

'Check! after about a dozen moves. It is of no use to go on; you always beat me. I should not mind that if I were any better now than when I started. It is not in me.'

'The reason is that you do not look two moves ahead. You never say to yourself, "Suppose I move there, what is she likely to do, and what can I do afterwards?"'

'That is just what is impossible to me. I cannot hold myself down; the moment I go beyond the next move my thoughts fly away, and I am in a muddle, and my head turns round. I was not born for it. I can do what is under my nose well enough, but nothing more.'

'The planning and the forecasting are the soul of the game. I should like to be a general, and play against armies and calculate the consequences of manœuvres.'

'It would kill me. I should prefer the fighting. Besides, calculation is useless, for when I think that you will be sure to move such and such a piece, you generally do not.'

'Then what makes the difference between the good and the bad player?'

'It is a gift, an instinct, I suppose.'

'Which is as much as to say that you give it up. You are very fond of that word instinct; I wish you would not use it.'

'I have heard you use it, and say you instinctively like this person or that.'

'Certainly; I do not deny that sometimes I am drawn to a person or repelled from him before I can say why; but I always force myself to discover afterwards the cause of my attraction or repulsion, and I believe it is a duty to do so. If we neglect it we are little better than the brutes, and may grossly deceive ourselves.'

At this moment the sound of wheels was heard, and Madge jumped up, nearly oversetting the board, and rushed into the front room. It was the four-horse coach from London, which, once a day, passed through Fenmarket on its road to Lincoln. It was not the direct route from London to Lincoln, but the *Defiance* went this way to accommodate Fenmarket and other small towns. It slackened speed in order to change horses at the Crown and Sceptre, and as Madge stood at the window, a gentleman on the box-seat looked at her intently as he passed. In another minute he had descended, and was welcomed by the landlord, who stood on the pavement. Clara meanwhile had taken up a book, but before she had read a page, her sister skipped into the parlour again, humming a tune.

'Let me see – check, you said, but it is not mate.'

She put her elbows on the table, rested her head between her hands, and appeared to contemplate the game profoundly.

'Now, then, what do you say to that?'

It was really a very lucky move, and Clara, whose thoughts perhaps were elsewhere, was presently most unaccountably defeated. Madge was triumphant.

'Where are all your deep-laid schemes? Baffled by a poor creature who can hardly put two and two together.'

'Perhaps your schemes were better than mine.'

'You know they were not. I saw the queen ought to take that bishop, and never bothered myself as to what would follow. Have you not lost your faith in schemes?'

'You are very much mistaken if you suppose that, because of one failure, or of twenty failures, I would give up a principle.'

'Clara, you are a strange creature. Don't let us talk any more about chess.'

Madge swept all the pieces with her hand into the box, shut it, closed the board, and put her feet on the fender.

'You never believe in impulses or in doing a thing just because here and now it appears to be the proper thing to do. Suppose anybody were to make love to you – oh! how I wish somebody would, you dear girl, for nobody deserves it more – ' Madge put her head caressingly on Clara's shoulder and then raised it again. 'Suppose, I say, anybody were to make love to you, would you hold off for six months and consider, and consider, and ask yourself whether he had such and such virtues, and whether he could make you happy? Would not that stifle love altogether? Would you not rather obey your first impression and, if you felt you loved him, would you not say "Yes"?'

'Time is not everything. A man who is prompt and is therefore thought to be hasty by sluggish creatures who are never half awake, may in five minutes spend more time in consideration than his critics will spend in as many weeks. I have never had the chance, and am not likely to have it. I can only say that if it were to come to me, I should try to use the whole strength of my soul. Precisely because the question would be so important, would it be necessary to employ every faculty I have in order to decide it. I do not believe in oracles which are supposed to prove their divinity by giving no reasons for their commands.'

'Ah, well, I believe in Shakespeare. His lovers fall in love at first sight.'

'No doubt they do, but to justify yourself you have to suppose that you are a Juliet and your friend a Romeo. They may, for aught I know, be examples in my favour. However, I have to lay down a rule for my own poor, limited self, and, to speak the truth, I am afraid that great men often do harm by imposing on us that which is serviceable to themselves only; or, to put it perhaps more correctly, we mistake the real nature of their processes, just as a person who is unskilled in arithmetic would mistake the processes of anybody who is very quick at it, and would be led away by them. Shakespeare is much to me, but the more he is to me, the more careful I ought to be to discover what is the true law of my own nature, more important to me after all than Shakespeare's.'

'Exactly. I know what the law of mine is. If a man were to present himself to me, I should rely on that instinct you so much despise, and I am certain that the balancing, see-saw method would be fatal. It would disclose a host of reasons against any conclusion, and I should never come to any.'

Clara smiled. Although this impetuosity was foreign to her, she loved it for the good which accompanied it.

'You do not mean to say you would accept or reject him at once?'

'No, certainly not. What I mean is that in a few days, perhaps in a shorter time, something within me would tell me whether we were suited to one another, although we might not have talked upon half-a-dozen subjects.'

'I think the risk tremendous.'

'But there is just as much risk the other way. You would examine your friend, catalogue him, sum up his beliefs, note his behaviour under various experimental trials, and miserably fail, after all your scientific investigation, to ascertain just the one important point whether you loved him and could live with him. Your reason was not meant for that kind of work. If a woman trusts in such matters to the faculty by which, when she wishes to settle whether she is to take this house or that, she puts the advantages of the larger back kitchen on one side and the bigger front kitchen on the other, I pity her.'

Mrs Hopgood at this moment came downstairs and asked when in the name of fortune they meant to have the tea ready.

CHAPTER 4

Frank Palmer, the gentleman whom we saw descend from the coach, was the eldest son of a wholesale and manufacturing chemist in London. He was now about five-and-twenty, and having just been admitted as a partner, he had begun, as the custom was in those days, to travel for his firm. The elder Mr Palmer was a man of refinement, something more than a Whig in politics, and an enthusiastic member of the Broad Church party, which was then becoming a power in the country. He was well-to-do, living in a fine old red-brick house at Stoke Newington, with half-a-dozen acres of ground round it, and, if Frank had been born thirty years later, he would probably have gone to Cambridge or Oxford. In those days, however, it was not the custom to send boys to the Universities, unless they were intended for the law, divinity or idleness, and Frank's training, which was begun at St Paul's school, was completed there. He lived at home, going to school in the morning and returning in the evening. He was surrounded by every influence which was pure and noble. Mr Maurice* and Mr Sterling* were his father's guests, and hence it may be inferred that there was an altar in the house, and that the sacred flame burnt thereon. Mr Palmer almost worshipped Mr Maurice, and his admiration was not blind, for Maurice connected the Bible with what was rational in his friend. 'What! still believable: no need then to pitch it overboard: here after all is the Eternal Word!' It can be imagined how those who dared not close their eyes to the light, and yet clung to that book which had been so much to their forefathers and themselves, rejoiced when they were able to declare that it belonged to them more than to those who misjudged them and could deny that they were heretics. The boy's education was entirely classical and athletic, and as he was quick at learning and loved his games, he took a high position amongst his schoolfellows. He was not particularly reflective, but he was generous and courageous, perfectly straightforward, a fair specimen of thousands of English public-school boys. As he grew up, he somewhat disappointed his father by a lack of any real interest in the subjects in which his father was interested. He accepted willingly, and even enthusiastically, the household conclusions on religion and politics, but they were not properly his, for he accepted them merely as conclusions and without the premisses, and it was often even a little annoying to hear him

express some free opinion on religious questions in a way which
showed that it was not a growth but something picked up. Mr
Palmer, senior, sometimes recoiled into intolerance and orthodoxy, and bewildered his son who, to use one of his own
phrases, 'hardly knew where his father was'. Partly the reaction
was due to the oscillation which accompanies serious and
independent thought, but mainly it was caused by Mr Palmer's
discontent with Frank's appropriation of a sentiment or doctrine
of which he was not the lawful owner. Frank, however, was so
hearty, so affectionate, and so cheerful, that it was impossible
not to love him dearly.

In his visits to Fenmarket, Frank had often noticed Madge,
for the Crown and Sceptre was his headquarters, and Madge
was well enough aware that she had been noticed. He had
inquired casually who it was who lived next door, and when the
waiter told him the name, and that Mr Hopgood was formerly
the bank manager, Frank remembered that he had often heard
his father speak of a Mr Hopgood, a clerk in a bank in London,
as one of his best friends. He did not fail to ask his father about
this friend, and to obtain an introduction to the widow. He had
now brought it to Fenmarket, and within half an hour after he
had alighted, he had presented it.

Mrs Hopgood, of course, recollected Mr Palmer perfectly,
and the welcome to Frank was naturally very warm. It was
delightful to connect earlier and happier days with the present,
and she was proud in the possession of a relationship which had
lasted so long. Clara and Madge, too, were both excited and
pleased. To say nothing of Frank's appearance, of his unsnob-
bish, deferential behaviour which showed that he understood
who they were and that the little house made no difference to
him, the girls and the mother could not resist a side glance at
Fenmarket and the indulgence of a secret satisfaction that it
would soon hear that the son of Mr Palmer, so well known in
every town round about, was on intimate terms with them.

Madge was particularly gay that evening. The presence of
sympathetic people was always a powerful stimulus to her, and
she was often astonished at the witty things and even the wise

things she said in such company, although, when she was alone, so few things wise or witty occurred to her. Like all persons who, in conversation, do not so much express the results of previous conviction obtained in silence as the inspiration of the moment, Madge dazzled everybody by a brilliancy which would have been impossible if she had communicated that which had been slowly acquired, but what she left with those who listened to her, did not always seem, on reflection, to be so much as it appeared to be while she was talking. Still she was very charming, and it must be confessed that sometimes her spontaneity was truer than the limitations of speech more carefully weighed.

'What makes you stay in Fenmarket, Mrs Hopgood? How I wish you would come to London!'

'I do not wish to leave it now; I have become attached to it; I have very few friends in London, and lastly, perhaps the most convincing reason, I could not afford it. Rent and living are cheaper here than in town.'

'Would you not like to live in London, Miss Hopgood?'

Clara hesitated for a few seconds.

'I am not sure – certainly not by myself. I was in London once for six months as a governess in a very pleasant family, where I saw much society; but I was glad to return to Fenmarket.'

'To the scenery round Fenmarket,' interrupted Madge; 'it is so romantic, so mountainous, so interesting in every way.'

'I was thinking of people, strange as it may appear. In London nobody really cares for anybody, at least, not in the sense in which I should use the words. Men and women in London stand for certain talents, and are valued often very highly for them, but they are valued merely as representing these talents. Now, if I had a talent, I should not be satisfied with admiration or respect because of it. No matter what admiration, or respect, or even enthusiasm I might evoke, even if I were told that my services had been immense and that life had been changed through my instrumentality, I should feel the lack of quiet, personal affection, and that, I believe, is not common in London. If I were famous, I would sacrifice all the adoration of the world for the love of a brother – if I had one – or a sister, who perhaps had never heard what it was which had made me renowned.'

'Certainly,' said Madge, laughing, 'for the love of *such* a sister. But, Mr Palmer, I like London. I like the people, just the people, although I do not know a soul, and not a soul cares a brass farthing about me. I am not half so stupid in London as in the country. I never have a thought of my own down here. How should I? But in London there is plenty of talk about all kinds of things, and I find I too have something in me. It is true, as Clara says, that nobody is anything particular to anybody, but that to me is rather pleasant. I do not want too much of profound and eternal attachments. They are rather a burden. They involve profound and eternal attachment on my part; and I have always to be at my best; such watchfulness and such jealousy! I prefer a dressing-gown and slippers and bonds which are not so tight.'

'Madge, Madge, I wish you would sometimes save me the trouble of laboriously striving to discover what you really mean.'

Mrs Hopgood bethought herself that her daughters were talking too much to one another, as they often did, even when guests were present, and she therefore interrupted them.

'Mr Palmer, you see both town and country – which do you prefer?'

'Oh! I hardly know; the country in summer-time, perhaps, and town in the winter.'

This was a safe answer, and one which was not very original; that is to say, it expressed no very distinct belief; but there was one valid reason why he liked being in London in the winter.

'Your father, I remember, loves music. I suppose you inherit his taste, and it is impossible to hear good music in the country.'

'I am very fond of music. Have you heard "St Paul"?* I was at Birmingham when it was first performed in this country. Oh! it *is* lovely,' and he began humming *Be thou faithful unto death*.

Frank did really care for music. He went wherever good music was to be had; he belonged to a choral society and was in great request amongst his father's friends at evening entertainments. He could also play the piano, so far as to be able to accompany himself thereon. He sang to himself when he was travelling, and often murmured favourite airs when people around him were talking. He had lessons from an old Italian, a little, withered, shabby creature, who was not very proud of his pupil. 'He is a talent,' said the Signor, 'and he will amuse himself; good for a ballad at a party, but a musician? no!' and like all mere 'talents' Frank failed in his songs to give them just what is of most value – just that which separates an artistic performance from the vast region of well-meaning, respectable, but uninteresting commonplace. There was a curious lack in him also of correspondence between his music and the rest of himself. As music is expression, it might be supposed that something which it serves to express would always lie behind it; but this was not the case with him, although he was so attractive and delightful in many ways. There could be no doubt that his love for Beethoven was genuine, but that which was in Frank Palmer was not that of which the sonatas and symphonies of the master are the voice. He went into raptures over the slow movement in the *C minor* Symphony,* but no *C minor* slow movement was discernible in his character.

'What on earth can be found in "St Paul" which can be put to music?' said Madge. 'Fancy a chapter in the Epistle to the Romans turned into a duet!'

'Madge! Madge! I am ashamed of you,' said her mother.

'Well, mother,' said Clara, 'I am sure that some of the settings by your divinity, Handel, are absurd. *For as in Adam all die* may be true enough, and the harmonies are magnificent, but I am always tempted to laugh when I hear it.'

Frank hummed the familiar apostrophe *Be not afraid.*

'Is that a bit of "St Paul"?' said Mrs Hopgood.

'Yes, it goes like this,' and Frank went up to the little piano and sang the song through.

'There is no fault to be found with that,' said Madge, 'so far as the coincidence of sense and melody is concerned, but I do not care much for oratorios. Better subjects can be obtained outside the Bible, and the main reason for selecting the Bible is that what is called religious music may be provided for good people. An oratorio, to me, is never quite natural. Jewish history is not a musical subject, and, besides, you cannot have proper love songs in an oratorio, and in them music is at its best.'

Mrs Hopgood was accustomed to her daughter's extravagance, but she was, nevertheless, a little uncomfortable.

'Ah!' said Frank, who had not moved from the piano, and he struck the first two bars of *Adelaide*.*

'Oh, please,' said Madge, 'go on, go on,' but Frank could not quite finish it.

She was sitting on the little sofa, and she put her feet up, lay and listened with her eyes shut. There was a vibration in Mr Palmer's voice not perceptible during his vision of the crown of life and of fidelity to death.

'Are you going to stay over Sunday?' inquired Mrs Hopgood.

'I am not quite sure; I ought to be back on Sunday evening. My father likes me to be at home on that day.'

'Is there not a Mr Maurice who is a friend of your father?'

'Oh, yes, a great friend.'

'He is not High Church nor Low Church?'

'No, not exactly.'

'What is he, then? What does he believe?'

'Well, I can hardly say; he does not believe that anybody will be burnt in a brimstone lake for ever.'

'That is what he does not believe,' interposed Clara.

'He believes that Socrates and the great Greeks and Romans who acted up to the light that was within them were not sent to hell. I think that is glorious, don't you?'

'Yes, but that also is something he does not believe. What is there in him which is positive? What has he distinctly won from the unknown?'

'Ah, Miss Hopgood, you ought to hear him yourself; he is wonderful. I do admire him so much; I am sure you would like him.'

'If you do not go home on Saturday,' said Mrs Hopgood, 'we shall be pleased if you will have dinner with us on Sunday; we generally go for a walk in the afternoon.'

Frank hesitated, but at that moment Madge rose from the

and he observed that she was tired and strange in her manner, although she was not ill, or, at least, not so ill as he had often before seen her. The few purchases they had to make at the draper's were completed, and they went out into the street. He took her hand-bag, and, in doing so, it opened and he saw to his horror a white silk pocket-handkerchief crumpled up in it, which he instantly recognised as one which had been shown him five minutes before, but he had not bought. The next moment a hand was on his shoulder. It was that of an assistant, who requested that they would both return for a few minutes. As they walked the half dozen steps back, the father's resolution was taken. "I am sixty," he thought to himself, "and she is fourteen." They went into the counting-house and he confessed that he had taken the handkerchief, but that it was taken by mistake and that he was about to restore it when he was arrested. The poor girl was now herself again, but her mind was an entire blank as to what she had done, and she could not doubt her father's statement, for it was a man's handkerchief and the bag was in his hands. The draper was inexorable, and as he had suffered much from petty thefts of late, had determined to make an example of the first offender whom he could catch. The father was accordingly prosecuted, convicted and sentenced to imprisonment. When his term had expired, his daughter, who, I am glad to say, never for an instant lost her faith in him, went away with him to a distant part of the country, where they lived under an assumed name. About ten years afterwards he died and kept his secret to the last; but he had seen the complete recovery and happy marriage of his child. It was remarkable that it never occurred to her that she might have been guilty, but her father's confession, as already stated, was apparently so sincere that she could do nothing but believe him. You will wonder how the facts were discovered. After his death a sealed paper disclosing them was found, with the inscription, "*Not to be opened during my daughter's life, and if she should have children or a husband who may survive her, it is to be burnt.*" She had no children, and when she died as an old woman, her husband also being dead, the seal was broken.'

'Probably,' said Madge, 'nobody except his daughter believed he was not a thief. For her sake he endured the imputation of common larceny, and was content to leave the world with only a remote chance that he would ever be justified.'

'I wonder,' said Frank, 'that he did not admit that it was his daughter who had taken the handkerchief, and excuse her on the ground of her ailment.'

'He could not do that,' replied Madge. 'The object of his life was to make as little of the ailment as possible. What would have been the effect on her if she had been made aware of its fearful consequences? Furthermore, would he have been believed? And then – awful thought, the child might have suspected him of attempting to shield himself at her expense! Do you think you could be capable of such sacrifice, Mr Palmer?'

Frank hesitated. 'It would – '

'The question is not fair, Madge,' said Mrs Hopgood, interrupting him. 'You are asking for a decision when all the materials to make up a decision are not present. It is wrong to question ourselves in cold blood as to what we should do in a great strait; for the emergency brings the insight and the power necessary to deal with it. I often fear lest, if such-and-such a trial were to befall me, I should miserably fail. So I should, furnished as I now am, but not as I should be under stress of the trial.'

'What is the use,' said Clara, 'of speculating whether we can, or cannot, do this or that? It *is* now an interesting subject for discussion whether the lie was a sin.'

'No,' said Madge, 'a thousand times no.'

'Brief and decisive. Well, Mr Palmer, what do you say?'

'That is rather an awkward question. A lie is a lie.'

'But not,' broke in Madge, vehemently, 'to save anybody whom you love. Is a contemptible little two-foot measuring-tape to be applied to such an action as that?'

'The consequences of such a philosophy, though, my dear,' said Mrs Hopgood, 'are rather serious. The moment you dispense with a fixed standard, you cannot refuse permission to other people to dispense with it also.'

'Ah, yes, I know all about that, but I am not going to give up my instinct for the sake of a rule. Do what you feel to be right, and let the rule go hang. Somebody, cleverer in logic than we are, will come along afterwards and find a higher rule which we have obeyed, and will formulate it concisely.'

'As for my poor self,' said Clara, 'I do not profess to know, without the rule, what is right and what is not. We are always trying to transcend the rule by some special pleading, and often in virtue of some fancied superiority. Generally speaking, the attempt is fatal.'

'Madge,' said Mrs Hopgood, 'your dogmatic decision may have been interesting, but it prevented the expression of Mr Palmer's opinion.'

Madge bent forward and politely inclined her head to the embarrassed Frank.

'I do not know what to say. I have never thought much about such matters. Is not what they call casuistry a science among Roman Catholics? If I were in a difficulty and could not tell right from wrong, I should turn Catholic, and come to you as my priest, Mrs Hopgood.'

'Then you would do, not what you thought right yourself, but what I thought right. The worth of the right to you is that it is your right, and that you arrive at it in your own way. Besides, you might not have time to consult anybody. Were you never compelled to settle promptly a case of this kind?'

'I remember once at school, when the mathematical master was out of the class-room, a boy named Carpenter ran up to the blackboard and wrote "Carrots" on it. That was the master's nickname, for he was red-haired. Scarcely was the word finished, when Carpenter heard him coming along the passage. There was just time partially to rub out some of the big letters, but CAR remained, and Carpenter was standing at the board when "Carrots" came in. He was an excitable man, and he knew very well what the boys called him.

' "What have you been writing on the board, sir?"

' "Carpenter, sir."

'The master examined the board. The upper half of the second

R was plainly perceptible, but it might possibly have been a P. He turned round, looked steadily at Carpenter for a moment, and then looked at us. Carpenter was no favourite, but not a soul spoke.

'"Go to your place, sir."

'Carpenter went to his place, the letters were erased and the lesson was resumed. I was greatly perplexed; I had acquiesced in a cowardly falsehood. Carrots was a great friend of mine, and I could not bear to feel that he was humbugged, so when we were outside I went up to Carpenter and told him he was an infernal sneak, and we had a desperate fight, and I licked him, and blacked both his eyes. I did not know what else to do.'

The company laughed.

'We cannot,' said Madge, 'all of us come to terms after this fashion with our consciences, but we have had enough of these discussions on morality. Let us go out.'

They went out, and, as some relief from the straight road, they turned into a field as they came home, and walked along a footpath which crossed the broad, deep ditches by planks. They were within about fifty yards of the last and broadest ditch, more a dyke than a ditch, when Frank, turning round, saw an ox, which they had not noticed, galloping after them.

'Go on, go on,' he cried, 'make for the plank.'

He discerned in an instant that unless the course of the animal could be checked it would overtake them before the bridge could be reached. The women fled, but Frank remained. He was in the habit of carrying a heavy walking-stick, the end of which he had hollowed out in his schooldays and had filled up with lead. Just as the ox came upon him, it laid its head to the ground, and Frank, springing aside, dealt it a tremendous, two-handed blow on the forehead with his knobbed weapon. The creature was dazed, it stopped and staggered, and in another instant Frank was across the bridge in safety. There was a little hysterical sobbing, but it was soon over.

'Oh, Mr Palmer,' said Mrs Hopgood, 'what presence of mind and what courage! We should have been killed without you.'

'The feat is not original, Mrs Hopgood. I saw it done by a

tough little farmer last summer on a bull that was really mad. There was no ditch for him though, poor fellow, and he had to jump a hedge.'

'You did not find it difficult,' said Madge, 'to settle your problem when it came to you in the shape of a wild ox.'

'Because there was nothing to settle,' said Frank, laughing; 'there was only one thing to be done.'

'So you believed, or rather, so you saw,' said Clara. 'I should have seen half-a-dozen things at once – that is to say, nothing.'

'And I,' said Madge, 'should have settled it the wrong way: I am sure I should, even if I had been a man. I should have bolted.'

Frank stayed to tea, and the evening was musical. He left about ten, but just as the door had shut he remembered he had forgotten his stick. He gave a gentle rap and Madge appeared. She gave him his stick.

'Goodbye again. Thanks for my life.'

Frank cursed himself that he could not find the proper word. He knew there was something which might be said and ought to be said, but he could not say it. Madge held out her hand to him, he raised it to his lips and kissed it, and then, astonished at his boldness, he instantly retreated. He went to the Crown and Sceptre and was soon in bed, but not to sleep. Strange, that the moment we lie down in the dark, images, which were half obscured, should become so intensely luminous! Madge hovered before Frank with almost tangible distinctness, and he felt his fingers moving in her heavy, voluptuous tresses. Her picture at last became almost painful to him and shamed him, so that he turned over from side to side to avoid it. He had never been thrown into the society of women of his own age, for he had no sister, and a fire was kindled within him which burnt with a heat all the greater because his life had been so pure. At last he fell asleep and did not wake till late in the morning. He had just time to eat his breakfast, pay one more business visit in the town, and catch the coach due at eleven o'clock from Lincoln to London. As the horses were being changed, he walked as near as he dared venture to the windows of the cottage next door, but he could see nobody. When the coach, however, began to move, he turned round and looked behind him, and a hand was waved to him. He took off his hat, and in five minutes he was clear of the town. It was in sight a long way, but when, at last, it disappeared, a cloud of wretchedness swept over him as the vapour sweeps up from the sea. What was she doing? talking to other people, existing for others, laughing with others! There were miles between himself and Fenmarket. Life! what was life? A few moments of living and long, dreary gaps between. All this, however, is a vain attempt to delineate what was shapeless. It was an intolerable, unvanquishable oppression. This was Love; this was the blessing which the god with the ruddy wings had bestowed on him. It was a relief to him when the coach rattled through Islington, and in a few minutes had landed him at the 'Angel'.

CHAPTER 6

There was to be a grand entertainment in the assembly room of the Crown and Sceptre in aid of the County Hospital. Mrs Martin, widow of one of the late partners in the bank, lived in a large house near Fenmarket, and still had an interest in the business. She was distinctly above anybody who lived in the town, and she knew how to show her superiority by venturing sometimes to do what her urban neighbours could not possibly do. She had been known to carry through the street a quart bottle of horse physic although it was wrapped up in nothing but brown paper. On her way she met the brewer's wife, who was more aggrieved than she was when Mrs Martin's carriage swept past her in the dusty, narrow lane which led to the Hall. Mrs Martin could also afford to recognise in a measure the claims of education and talent. A gentleman came from London to lecture in the town, and showed astonished Fenmarket an orrery* and a magic lantern with dissolving views of the Holy

Land. The exhibition had been provided in order to extinguish
a debt incurred in repairing the church, but the rector's wife,
and the brewer's wife, after consultation, decided that they must
leave the lecturer to return to his inn. Mrs Martin, however,
invited him to supper. Of course she knew Mr Hopgood well,
and knew that he was no ordinary man. She knew also something of Mrs Hopgood and the daughters, and that they were
no ordinary women. She had been heard to say that they were
ladies, and that Mr Hopgood was a gentleman; and she kept up
a distant kind of intimacy with them, always nodded to them
whenever she met them, and every now and then sent them
grapes and flowers. She had observed once or twice to Mrs
Tubbs that Mr Hopgood was a remarkable person, who was
quite scientific and therefore did not associate with the rest of
the Fenmarket folk; and Mrs Tubbs was much annoyed, particularly by a slight emphasis which she thought she detected in the
'therefore', for Mr Tubbs had told her that one of the smaller
London brewers, who had only about fifty public-houses, had
refused to meet at dinner a learned French chemist who had
written books. Mrs Martin could not make friends with the
Hopgoods, nor enter the cottage. It would have been a transgres-
sion of that infinitely fine and tortuous line whose inexplicable
convolutions mark off what is forbidden to a society lady.
Clearly, however, the Hopgoods could be requested to co-
operate at the Crown and Sceptre; in fact, it would be impolitic
not to put some of the townsfolk on the list of patrons. So it
came about that Mrs Hopgood was included, and that she was
made responsible for the provision of one song and one recitation. For the song it was settled that Frank Palmer should be
asked, as he would be in Fenmarket. Usually he came but once
every half year, but he had not been able, so he said, to finish all
his work the last time. The recitation Madge undertook.

The evening arrived, the room was crowded and a dozen
private carriages stood in the Crown and Sceptre courtyard.
Frank called for the Hopgoods. Mrs Hopgood and Clara sat
with presentation tickets in the second row, amongst the
fashionable folk; Frank and Madge were upon the platform.

Frank was loudly applauded in *Il Mio Tesoro*,* but the loudest applause of the evening was reserved for Madge, who declaimed Byron's *Destruction of Sennacherib** with much energy. She certainly looked very charming in her red gown, harmonising with her black hair. The men in the audience were vociferous for something more, and would not be contented until she again came forward. The truth is, that the wily young woman had prepared herself beforehand for possibilities, but she artfully concealed her preparation. Looking on the ground and hesitating, she suddenly raised her head as if she had just remembered something, and then repeated Sir Henry Wotton's *Happy Life.** She was again greeted with cheers, subdued so as to be in accordance with the character of the poem, but none the less sincere, and in the midst of them she gracefully bowed and retired. Mrs Martin complimented her warmly at the end of the performance, and inwardly debated whether Madge could be asked to enliven one of the parties at the Hall, and how it could, at the same time, be made clear to the guests that she and her mother, who must come with her, were not even acquaintances, properly so called, but were patronised as persons of merit living in the town which the Hall protected. Mrs Martin was obliged to be very careful. She certainly was on the list at the Lord Lieutenant's, but she was in the outer ring, and she was not asked to those small and select little dinners which were given to Sir Egerton, the Dean of Peterborough, Lord Francis, and his brother, the county member. She decided, however, that she could make perfectly plain the conditions upon which the Hopgoods would be present, and the next day she sent Madge a little note asking her if she would 'assist in some festivities' at the Hall in about two months' time, which were to be given in celebration of the twenty-first birthday of Mrs Martin's third son. The scene from the *Tempest*, where Ferdinand and Miranda are discovered playing chess,* was suggested, and it was proposed that Madge should be Miranda, and Mr Palmer Ferdinand. Mrs Martin concluded with a hope that Mrs Hopgood and her eldest daughter would 'witness the performance'.

Frank joyously consented, for amateur theatricals had always

attracted him, and in a few short weeks he was again at
Fenmarket. He was obliged to be there for three or four days
before the entertainment, in order to attend the rehearsals,
which Mrs Martin had put under the control of a professional
gentleman from London, and Madge and he were consequently
compelled to make frequent journeys to the Hall.

At last the eventful night arrived, and a carriage was hired
next door to take the party. They drove up to the grand entrance
and were met by a footman, who directed Madge and Frank to
their dressing-rooms, and escorted Mrs Hopgood and Clara to
their places in the theatre. They had gone early in order to
accommodate Frank and Madge, and they found themselves
alone. They were surprised that there was nobody to welcome
them, and a little more surprised when they found that the
places allotted to them were rather in the rear. Presently two or
three fiddlers were seen, who began to tune their instruments.
Then some Fenmarket folk and some of the well-to-do tenants
on the estate made their appearance, and took seats on either
side of Mrs Hopgood and Clara. Quite at the back were the
servants. At five minutes to eight the band struck up the overture
to *Zampa*,* and in the midst of it in sailed Mrs Martin and a
score or two of fashionably-dressed people, male and female.
The curtain ascended and Prospero's cell was seen. Alonso and
his companions were properly grouped, and Prospero began,—

> Behold, Sir King,
> The wronged Duke of Milan, Prospero.*

The audience applauded him vigorously when he came to the
end of his speech, but there was an instantaneous cry of 'hush!'
when Prospero disclosed the lovers. It was really very pretty.
Miranda wore a loose, simple, white robe, and her wonderful
hair was partly twisted into a knot, and partly strayed down to
her waist. The dialogue between the two was spoken with much
dramatic feeling, and when Ferdinand came to the lines—

> Sir, she is mortal,
> But by immortal Providence she's mine,*

old Boston, a worthy and wealthy farmer, who sat next to Mrs Hopgood, cried out 'hear, hear!' but was instantly suppressed. He put his head down behind the people in front of him, rubbed his knees, grinned, and then turned to Mrs Hopgood, whom he knew, and whispered, with his hand to his mouth, –

'And a precious lucky chap he is.'

Mrs Hopgood watched intently, and when Gonzalo invoked the gods to drop a blessed crown on the couple,* and the applause was renewed, and Boston again cried 'hear, hear!' without fear of check, she did not applaud, for something told her that behind this stage show a drama was being played of far more serious importance.

The curtain fell, but there were loud calls for the performers. It rose, and they presented themselves, Alonso still holding the hands of the happy pair. The cheering now was vociferous, more particularly when a wreath was flung at the feet of the young princess, and Ferdinand, stooping, placed it on her head.

Again the curtain fell, the band struck up some dance music and the audience were treated to 'something light', and roared with laughter at a pretty chambermaid at an inn who captivated and bamboozled a young booby who was staying there, pitched him overboard; 'wondered what he meant'; sang an audacious song recounting her many exploits, and finished with a *pas-seul*.

The performers and their friends were invited to a sumptuous supper, and the Fenmarket folk were not at home until half-past two in the morning. On their way back, Clara broke out against the juxtaposition of Shakespeare and such vulgarity.

'Much better,' she said, 'to have left the Shakespeare out altogether. The lesson of the sequence is that each is good in its way, a perfectly hateful doctrine to me.'

Frank and Madge were, however, in the best of humours, especially Frank, who had taken a glass of wine beyond his customary very temperate allowance.

'But, Miss Hopgood, Mrs Martin had to suit all tastes; we must not be too severe upon her.'

There was something in this remark most irritating to Clara; the word 'taste', for example, as if the difference between

Miranda and the chambermaid were a matter of 'taste'. She was
annoyed too with Frank's easy, cheery tones for she felt deeply
what she said, and his mitigation and smiling latitudinarianism
were more exasperating than direct opposition.

'I am sure,' continued Frank, 'that if we were to take the votes
of the audience, Miranda would be the queen of the evening';
and he put the crown which he had brought away with him on
her head again.

Clara was silent. In a few moments they were at the door of
their house. It had begun to rain, and Madge, stepping out of
the carriage in a hurry, threw a shawl over her head, forgetting
the wreath. It fell into the gutter and was splashed with mud.
Frank picked it up, wiped it as well as he could with his pocket-
handkerchief, took it into the parlour and laid it on a chair.

CHAPTER 7

The next morning it still rained, a cold rain from the north-east,
a very disagreeable type of weather on the Fenmarket flats.
Madge was not awake until late, and when she caught sight of
the grey sky and saw her finery tumbled on the floor – no further
use for it in any shape save as rags – and the dirty crown, which
she had brought upstairs, lying on the heap, the leaves already
fading, she felt depressed and miserable. The breakfast was dull,
and for the most part all three were silent. Mrs Hopgood and
Clara went away to begin their housework, leaving Madge alone.

'Madge,' cried Mrs Hopgood, 'what am I to do with this
thing? It is of no use to preserve it; it is dead and covered with
dirt.'

'Throw it down here.'

She took it and rammed it into the fire. At that moment she
saw Frank pass. He was evidently about to knock, but she ran
to the door and opened it.

'I did not wish to keep you waiting in the wet.'

'I am just off, but I could not help calling to see how you are. What! burning your laurels, the testimony to your triumph?'

'Triumph! rather transitory; finishes in smoke,' and she pushed two or three of the unburnt leaves amongst the ashes and covered them over. He stooped down, picked up a leaf, smoothed it between his fingers, and then raised his eyes. They met hers at that instant, as she lifted them and looked in his face. They were near one another, and his hands strayed towards hers till they touched. She did not withdraw; he clasped the hand, she not resisting; in another moment his arms were round her, his face was on hers, and he was swept into self-forgetfulness. Suddenly the horn of the coach about to start awoke him, and he murmured the line from one of his speeches of the night before –

> But by immortal Providence she's mine.

She released herself a trifle, held her head back as if she desired to survey him apart from her, so that the ecstasy of union might be renewed, and then fell on his neck.

The horn once more sounded, she let him out silently, and he was off. Mrs Hopgood and Clara presently came downstairs.

'Mr Palmer came in to bid you goodbye, but he heard the coach and was obliged to rush away.'

'What a pity,' said Mrs Hopgood, 'that you did not call us.'

'I thought he would be able to stay longer.'

The lines which followed Frank's quotation came into her head, –

> 'Sweet lord, you play me false.'
> 'No, my dearest love,
> I would not for the world.'*

'An omen,' she said to herself; ' "he would not for the world".'

She was in the best of spirits all day long. When the house-work was over and they were quiet together, she said, –

'Now, my dear mother and sister, I want to know how the performance pleased you.'

'It was as good as it could be,' replied her mother, 'but I cannot think why all plays should turn upon lovemaking. I wonder whether the time will ever come when we shall care for a play in which there is no courtship.'

'What a horrible heresy, mother,' said Madge.

'It may be so; it may be that I am growing old, but it seems astonishing to me sometimes that the world does not grow a little weary of endless variations on the same theme.'

'Never,' said Madge, 'as long as it does not weary of the thing itself, and it is not likely to do that. Fancy a young man and a young woman stopping short and exclaiming, "This is just what every son of Adam and daughter of Eve has gone through before; why should we proceed?" Besides, it is the one emotion common to the whole world; we can all comprehend it. Once more, it reveals character. In *Hamlet* and *Othello*, for example, what is interesting is not solely the bare love. The natures of Hamlet and Othello are brought to light through it as they would not have been through any other stimulus. I am sure that no ordinary woman ever shows what she really is, except when she is in love. Can you tell what she is from what she calls her religion, or from her friends, or even from her husband?'

'Would it not be equally just to say women are more alike in love than in anything else? Mind, I do not say alike, but more alike. Is it not the passion which levels us all?'

'Oh, mother, mother! did one ever hear such dreadful blasphemy? That the loves, for example, of two such cultivated, exquisite creatures as Clara and myself would be nothing different from those of the barmaids next door?'

'Well, at any rate, I do not want to see *my* children in love to understand what they are – to me at least.'

'Then, if you comprehend us so completely – and let us have no more philosophy – just tell me, should I make a good actress? Oh! to be able to sway a thousand human beings into tears or laughter! It must be divine.'

'No, I do not think you would,' replied Clara.

'Why not, miss? *Your* opinion, mind, was not asked. Did I not act to perfection last night?'

'Yes.'

'Then why are you so decisive?'

'Try a different part some day. I may be mistaken.'

'You are very oracular.'

She turned to the piano, played a few chords, closed the instrument, swung herself round on the music stool, and said she should go for a walk.

CHAPTER 8

It was Mr Palmer's design to send Frank abroad as soon as he understood the home trade. It was thought it would be an advantage to him to learn something of foreign manufacturing processes. Frank had gladly agreed to go, but he was now rather in the mood for delay. Mr Palmer conjectured a reason for it, and the conjecture was confirmed when, after two or three more visits to Fenmarket, perfectly causeless, so far as business was concerned, Frank asked for the paternal sanction to his engagement with Madge. Consent was willingly given, for Mr Palmer knew the family well; letters passed between him and Mrs Hopgood, and it was arranged that Frank's visit to Germany should be postponed till the summer. He was now frequently at Fenmarket as Madge's accepted suitor, and, as the spring advanced, their evenings were mostly spent by themselves out of doors. One afternoon they went for a long walk, and on their return they rested by a stile. Those were the days when Tennyson was beginning to stir the hearts of the young people in England, and the two little green volumes had just become a treasure in the Hopgood household. Mr Palmer, senior, knew them well, and Frank, hearing his father speak so enthusiastically about them, thought Madge would like them, and had presented them to her. He had heard one or two read aloud at home, and had looked at one or two himself, but had gone no further. Madge, her mother, and her sister had read and re-read them.

'Oh,' said Madge, 'for that Vale in Ida. Here in these fens how I long for something that is not level! Oh, for the roar of –

> The long brook falling thro' the clov'n ravine
> In cataract after cataract to the sea.*

Go on with it, Frank.'

'I cannot.'

'But you know *Œnone*?'

'I cannot say I do. I began it – '

'Frank, how could you begin it and lay it down unfinished? Besides, those lines are some of the first; you *must* remember –

> Behind the valley topmost Gargarus
> Stands up and takes the morning.'*

'No, I do not recollect, but I will learn them; learn them for your sake.'

'I do not want you to learn them for my sake.'

'But I shall.'

She had taken off her hat and his hand strayed to her neck. Her head fell on his shoulder and she had forgotten his ignorance of *Œnone*. Presently she awoke from her delicious trance and they moved homewards in silence. Frank was a little uneasy.

'I do greatly admire Tennyson,' he said.

'What do you admire? You have hardly looked at him.'

'I saw a very good review of him. I will look that review up, by the way, before I come down again. Mr Maurice was talking about it.'

Madge had a desire to say something, but she did not know what to say, a burden lay upon her chest. It was that weight which presses there when we are alone with those with whom we are not strangers, but with whom we are not completely at home, and she actually found herself impatient and half-desirous of solitude. This must be criminal or disease, she thought to herself, and she forcibly recalled Frank's virtues. She was so far successful that when they parted and he kissed her, she was more than usually caressing, and her ardent embrace, at least for the moment, relieved that unpleasant sensation in the region of the heart. When he had gone she reasoned with herself. What a miserable counterfeit of love, she argued, is mere intellectual sympathy, a sympathy based on books! What did Miranda know about Ferdinand's 'views' on this or that subject? Love is something independent of 'views'. It is an attraction which has always been held to be inexplicable, but whatever it may be it is not 'views'. She was becoming a little weary, she thought, of what was called 'culture'. These creatures whom we know through Shakespeare and Goethe are ghostly. What have we to do with them? It is idle work to read or even to talk fine things about them. It ends in nothing. What we really have to go through and that which goes through it are interesting, but not circumstances and character impossible to us. When Frank spoke of his business, which he understood, he was wise, and some observations which he made the other day, on the management of his workpeople, would have been thought original if they had been printed. The true artist knows that his hero must be a character shaping events and shaped by them, and not a babbler about literature. Frank, also, was so susceptible. He liked to hear her read to him, and her enthusiasm would soon be his. Moreover, how gifted he was, unconsciously, with all that makes a man admirable, with courage, with perfect unselfishness! How handsome he was, and then his passion for her! She had read something of passion, but she never knew till now what the white intensity of its flame in a man could be. She was committed, too, happily committed; it was an engagement.

Thus, whenever doubt obtruded itself, she poured a self-raised tide over it and concealed it. Alas! it could not be washed away; it was a little sharp rock based beneath the ocean's depths, and when the water ran low its dark point reappeared. She was more successful, however, than many women would have been, for, although her interest in ideas was deep, there was fire in her blood, and Frank's arm around her made the world well nigh disappear; her surrender was entire, and if Sinai had thundered in her ears she would not have heard. She was destitute of that power, which her sister possessed, of surveying herself from a distance. On the contrary, her emotion enveloped her, and the safeguard of reflection on it was impossible to her.

As to Frank, no doubt ever approached him. He was intoxicated, and beside himself. He had been brought up in a clean household, knowing nothing of the vice by which so many young men are overcome, and woman hitherto had been a mystery to him. Suddenly he found himself the possessor of a beautiful creature, whose lips it was lawful to touch and whose heartbeats he could feel as he pressed her to his breast. It was permitted him to be alone with her, to sit on the floor and rest his head on her knees, and he had ventured to capture one of her slippers and carry it off to London, where he kept it locked up amongst his treasures. If he had been drawn over Fenmarket sluice in a winter flood he would not have been more incapable of resistance.

Every now and then Clara thought she discerned in Madge that she was not entirely content, but the cloud-shadows swept past so rapidly and were followed by such dazzling sunshine that she was perplexed and hoped that her sister's occasional moodiness might be due to parting and absence, or the anticipation of them. She never ventured to say anything about Frank to Madge, for there was something in her which forbade all approach from that side. Once when he had shown his ignorance of what was so familiar to the Hopgoods, and Clara had expected some sign of dissatisfaction from her sister, she appeared ostentatiously to champion him against anticipated criticism. Clara interpreted the warning and was silent, but, after she had left the room with her mother in order that the lovers might be alone, she went upstairs and wept many tears. Ah! it is a sad experience when the nearest and dearest suspects that we are aware of secret disapproval, knows that it is justifiable, throws up a rampart and becomes defensively belligerent. From that moment all confidence is at an end. Without a word, perhaps, the love and friendship of years disappear, and in the place of two human beings transparent to each other, there are two who are opaque and indifferent. Bitter, bitter! If the cause of separation were definite disagreement upon conduct or belief, we could pluck up courage, approach and come to an understanding, but it is impossible to bring to speech anything which is so close to the heart, and there is, therefore, nothing left for us but to submit and be dumb.

CHAPTER 9

It was now far into June, and Madge and Frank extended their walks and returned later. He had come down to spend his last Sunday with the Hopgoods before starting with his father for Germany, and on the Monday they were to leave London.

Wordsworth was one of the divinities at Stoke Newington, and just before Frank visited Fenmarket that week, he had heard the *Intimations of Immortality** read with great fervour. Thinking that Madge would be pleased with him if she found that he knew something about that famous Ode, and being really smitten with some of the passages in it, he learnt it, and just as they were about to turn homewards one sultry evening he suddenly began to repeat it, and declaimed it to the end with much rhetorical power.

'Bravo!' said Madge, 'but, of all Wordsworth's poems, that is the one for which I believe I care the least.'

Frank's countenance fell.

'Oh, me! I thought it was just what would suit you.'

'No, not particularly. There are some noble lines in it; for example –

> And custom lie upon thee with a weight,
> Heavy as frost, and deep almost as life!*

But the very title – *Intimations of Immortality from Recollections of Early Childhood* – is unmeaning to me, and as for the verse which is in everybody's mouth –

> Our birth is but a sleep and a forgetting;

and still worse the vision of "that immortal sea", and of the children who "sport upon the shore", they convey nothing whatever to me. I find though they are much admired by the clergy of the better sort, and by certain religiously-disposed people, to whom thinking is distasteful or impossible. Because they cannot definitely believe, they fling themselves with all the more fervour upon these cloudy Wordsworthian phrases, and imagine they see something solid in the coloured fog.'

It was now growing dark and a few heavy drops of rain began to fall, but in a minute or two they ceased. Frank, contrary to his usual wont, was silent. There was something undiscovered in Madge, a region which he had not visited and perhaps could not enter. She discerned in an instant what she had done, and in an instant repented. He had taken so much pains with a long piece of poetry for her sake: was not that better than agreement in a set of propositions? Scores of persons might think as she thought about the ode, who would not spend a moment in doing anything to gratify her. It was delightful also to reflect that Frank imagined she would sympathise with anything written in that temper. She recalled what she herself had said when somebody gave Clara a copy in 'Parian' of a Greek statue, a thing coarse in outline and vulgar. Clara was about to put it in a cupboard in the attic, but Madge had pleaded so pathetically that the donor had in a measure divined what her sister loved, and had done her best, although she had made a mistake, that finally the statue was placed on the bedroom mantelpiece. Madge's heart overflowed, and Frank had never attracted her so powerfully as at that moment. She took his hand softly in hers.

'Frank,' she murmured, as she bent her head towards him, 'it is really a lovely poem.'

Suddenly there was a flash of forked lightning at some distance, followed in a few seconds by a roll of thunder increasing in intensity until the last reverberation seemed to shake the ground. They took refuge in a little barn and sat down. Madge, who was timid and excited in a thunderstorm, closed her eyes to shield herself from the glare.

The tumult in the heavens lasted for nearly two hours and, when it was over, Madge and Frank walked homewards without speaking a word for a good part of the way.

'I cannot, cannot go tomorrow,' he suddenly cried, as they neared the town.

'You *shall* go,' she replied calmly.

'But, Madge, think of me in Germany, think what my dreams and thoughts will be – you here – hundreds of miles between us.'

She had never seen him so shaken with terror.

'You *shall* go; not another word.'

'I must say something – what can I say? My God, my God, have mercy on me!'

'Mercy! mercy!' she repeated, half unconsciously, and then rousing herself, exclaimed, 'You shall not say it; I will not hear; now, goodbye.'

They had come to the door; he went inside; she took his face between her hands, left one kiss on his forehead, led him back to the doorway and he heard the bolts drawn. When he recovered himself he went to the Crown and Sceptre and tried to write a letter to her, but the words looked hateful, horrible on the paper, and they were not the words he wanted. He dared not go near the house the next morning, but as he passed it on the coach he looked at the windows. Nobody was to be seen, and that night he left England.

'Did you hear,' said Clara to her mother at breakfast, 'that the lightning struck one of the elms in the avenue at Mrs Martin's yesterday evening and splintered it to the ground?'

CHAPTER 10

In a few days Madge received the following letter: –

Frankfort, O. M.,*
Hotel Waidenbusch

My dearest Madge, – I do not know how to write to you. I have begun a dozen letters but I cannot bring myself to speak of what lies before me, hiding the whole world from me. Forgiveness! how is any forgiveness possible? But Madge, my dearest Madge, remember that my love is intenser than ever. What has happened has bound you closer to me. I *implore* you to let me come back. I will find a thousand excuses for returning, and we will marry. We had vowed marriage to each other and why should not our vows be fulfilled? Marriage, marriage *at once*. You will not, you *cannot*, no, you *cannot*, you must see you cannot refuse. My father wishes to make this town his headquarters for ten days. Write by return for mercy's sake. – Your ever devoted

Frank

The reply came only a day late.

My dear Frank, – Forgiveness! Who is to be forgiven? Not you. You believed you loved me, but I doubted my love, and I know now that no true love for you exists. We must part, and part forever. Whatever wrong may have been done, marriage to avoid disgrace would be a wrong to both of us infinitely greater. I owe you an expiation; your release is all I can offer, and it is insufficient. I can only plead that I was deaf and blind. By some miracle, I cannot tell how, my ears and eyes are opened, and I hear and see. It is not the first time in my life that the truth has been revealed to me suddenly, supernaturally, I may say, as if in a vision, and I know the revelation is authentic. There must be no wavering, no half-measures, and I absolutely forbid another letter from you. If one arrives I must, for the sake of my own peace and resolution, refuse to read it. You have simply to announce to your father that the engagement is at an end, and give no reasons. – Your faithful friend

Madge Hopgood

Another letter did come, but Madge was true to her word, and it was returned unopened.

For a long time Frank was almost incapable of reflection. He dwelt on an event which might happen, but which he dared not name; and if it should happen! Pictures of his father, his home, his father's friends, Fenmarket, the Hopgood household, passed before him with such wild rapidity and intermingled complexity that it seemed as if the reins had dropped out of his hands and he was being hurried away to madness. He resisted with all his might this dreadful sweep of the imagination, tried to bring himself back into sanity and to devise schemes by which, although he was prohibited from writing to Madge, he might obtain news of her. Her injunction might not be final. There was but one hope for him, one possibility of extrication, one necessity – their marriage. It *must* be. He dared not think of what might be the consequences if they did not marry.

Hitherto Madge had given no explanation to her mother or sister of the rupture, but one morning – nearly two months had now passed – Clara did not appear at breakfast.

'Clara is not here,' said Mrs Hopgood; 'she was very tired last night, perhaps it is better not to disturb her.'

'Oh, no! please let her alone. I will see if she still sleeps.'

Madge went upstairs, opened her sister's door noiselessly, saw that she was not awake, and returned. When breakfast was over she rose, and after walking up and down the room once or twice, seated herself in the armchair by her mother's side. Her mother drew herself a little nearer, and took Madge's hand gently in her own.

'Madge, my child, have you nothing to say to your mother?'

'Nothing.'

'Cannot you tell me why Frank and you have parted? Do you not think I ought to know something about such an event in the life of one so close to me?'

'I broke off the engagement: we were not suited to one another.'

'I thought as much; I honour you; a thousand times better that you should separate now than find out your mistake afterwards when it is irrevocable. Thank God, He has given you such courage! But you must have suffered – I know you must;' and she tenderly kissed her daughter.

'Oh, mother! mother!' cried Madge, 'what is the worst – at least to you – you – the worst that can happen to a woman?'

Mrs Hopgood did not speak; something presented itself which she refused to recognise, but she shuddered. Before she could recover herself Madge broke out again, –

'It has happened to me; mother, your daughter has wrecked your peace for ever!'

'And he has abandoned you?'

'No, no; I told you it was I who left him.'

It was Mrs Hopgood's custom, when any evil news was suddenly communicated to her, to withdraw at once if possible to her own room. She detached herself from Madge, rose, and, without a word, went upstairs and locked her door. The struggle was terrible. So much thought, so much care, such an education, such noble qualities, and they had not accomplished what ordinary ignorant Fenmarket mothers and daughters were able to achieve! This fine life, then, was a failure, and a perfect example of literary and artistic training had gone the way of the common wenches whose affiliation cases figured in the county newspaper. She was shaken and bewildered. She was neither orthodox nor secular. She was too strong to be afraid that what she disbelieved could be true, and yet a fatal weakness had been disclosed in what had been set up as its substitute. She could not treat her child as a sinner who was to be tortured into something like madness by immitigable punishment, but, on the other hand, she felt that this sorrow was unlike other sorrows and that it could never be healed. For some time she was powerless, blown this way and that way by contradictory storms, and unable to determine herself to any point whatever. She was not, however, new to the tempest. She had lived and had survived when she thought she must have gone down. She had learned the wisdom which the passage through desperate straits can bring. At last she prayed and in a few minutes a message was whispered to her. She went into the breakfast-room and seated herself again by Madge. Neither uttered a word, but Madge fell down before her, and, with a great cry, buried her face in her mother's lap. She remained kneeling for some time waiting for a rebuke, but none came. Presently she felt smoothing hands on her head and the soft impress of lips. So was she judged.

It was settled that they should leave Fenmarket. Their departure caused but little surprise. They had scarcely any friends, and it was always conjectured that people so peculiar would ultimately find their way to London. They were particularly desirous to conceal their movements, and therefore determined to warehouse their furniture in town, to take furnished apartments there for three months, and then to move elsewhere. Any letters which might arrive at Fenmarket for them during these three months would be sent to them at their new address; nothing probably would come afterwards, and as nobody in Fenmarket would care to take any trouble about them, their trace would become obliterated. They found some rooms near Myddelton Square, Pentonville,* not a particularly cheerful place, but they wished to avoid a more distant suburb, and Pentonville was cheap. Fortunately for them they had no difficulty whatever in getting rid of the Fenmarket house for the remainder of their term.

For a little while London diverted them after a fashion, but the absence of household cares told upon them. They had nothing to do but to read and to take dismal walks through Islington and Barnsbury, and the gloom of the outlook thickened as the days became shorter and the smoke began to darken the air. Madge was naturally more oppressed than the others, not only by reason of her temperament, but because she was the author of the trouble which had befallen them. Her mother and Clara did everything to sustain and to cheer her. They possessed the rare virtue of continuous tenderness. The love, which with many is an inspiration, was with them their own selves, from which they could not be separated; a harsh word could not therefore escape from them. It was as impossible as that there should be any failure in the pressure with which the rocks press towards the earth's centre. Madge at times was very far gone in melancholy. How different this thing looked when it was close at hand; when she personally was to be the victim! She had read about it in history, the surface of which it seemed scarcely to ripple; it had been turned to music in some of her favourite poems and had lent a charm to innumerable mythologies, but the actual fact was nothing like the poetry or mythology, and threatened to ruin her own history altogether. Nor would it be her own history solely, but more or less that of her mother and sister.

Had she believed in the common creed, her attention would have been concentrated on the salvation of her own soul; she would have found her Redeemer and would have been comparatively at peace; she would have acknowledged herself convicted of infinite sin, and hell would have been opened before her, but above the sin and the hell she would have seen the distinct image of the Mediator abolishing both. Popular theology makes personal salvation of such immense importance that, in comparison therewith, we lose sight of the consequences to others of our misdeeds. The sense of cruel injustice to those who loved her remained with Madge perpetually.

To obtain relief she often went out of London for the day; sometimes her mother and sister went with her; sometimes she insisted on going alone. One autumn morning, she found herself at Letherhead, the longest trip she had undertaken, for there were scarcely any railways then. She wandered about till she discovered a footpath which took her to a mill-pond, which spread itself out into a little lake. It was fed by springs which burst up through the ground. She watched at one particular point, and saw the water boil up with such force that it cleared a space of a dozen yards in diameter from every weed, and formed a transparent pool just tinted with that pale azure which is peculiar to the living fountains which break out from the bottom of the chalk. She was fascinated for a moment by the spectacle, and reflected upon it, but she passed on. In about three-quarters of an hour she found herself near a church, larger than an ordinary village church, and, as she was tired, and the gate of the church porch was open, she entered and sat down.

The sun streamed in upon her, and some sheep which had strayed into the churchyard from the adjoining open field came almost close to her, unalarmed, and looked in her face. The quiet was complete, and the air so still, that a yellow leaf dropping here and there from the churchyard elms – just beginning to turn – fell quiveringly in a straight path to the earth. Sick at heart and despairing, she could not help being touched, and she thought to herself how strange the world is – so transcendent both in glory and horror; a world capable of such scenes as those before her, and a world in which such suffering as hers could be; a world infinite both ways. The porch gate was open because the organist was about to practise, and in another instant she was listening to the *Kyrie* from Beethoven's Mass in C.* She knew it; Frank had tried to give her some notion of it on the piano, and since she had been in London she had heard it at St Mary's, Moorfields.* She broke down and wept, but there was something new in her sorrow, and it seemed as if a certain Pity overshadowed her.

She had barely recovered herself when she saw a woman, apparently about fifty, coming towards her with a wicker basket on her arm. She sat down beside Madge, put her basket on the ground, and wiped her face with her apron.

'Marnin' miss! its rayther hot walkin', isn't it? I've come all the way from Darkin, and I'm goin' to Great Oakhurst. That's a longish step there and back again; not that this is the nearest way, but I don't like climbing them hills, and then when I get to Letherhead I shall have a lift in a cart.'

Madge felt bound to say something as the sunburnt face looked kind and motherly.

'I suppose you live at Great Oakhurst?'

'Yes. I do: my husband, God bless him! he was a kind of foreman at The Towers, and when he died I was left alone and didn't know what to be at, as both my daughters were out and one married; so I took the general shop at Great Oakhurst, as Longwood used to have, but it don't pay for I ain't used to it, and the house is too big for me, and there isn't nobody proper to mind it when I goes over to Darkin for anything.'

'Are you going to leave?'

'Well, I don't quite know yet, miss, but I thinks I shall live with my daughter in London. She's married a cabinetmaker in Great Ormond Street: they let lodgings, too. Maybe you know that part?'

'No, I do not.'

'You don't live in London, then?'

'Yes, I do. I came from London this morning.'

'The Lord have mercy on us, did you though! I suppose, then, you're a-visitin' here. I know most of the folk hereabouts.'

'No: I am going back this afternoon.'

Her interrogator was puzzled and her curiosity stimulated. Presently she looked in Madge's face.

'Ah! my poor dear, you'll excuse me, I don't mean to be forward, but I see you've been a-cryin': there's somebody buried here.'

'No.'

That was all she could say. The walk from Letherhead, and the excitement had been too much for her and she fainted. Mrs Caffyn, for that was her name, was used to fainting fits. She was often 'a bit faint' herself, and she instantly loosened Madge's gown, brought out some smelling-salts and also a little bottle of brandy and water. Something suddenly struck her. She took up Madge's hand: there was no wedding ring on it.

Presently her patient recovered herself.

'Look you now, my dear; you aren't noways fit to go back to London today. If you was my child you shouldn't do it for all the gold in the Indies, no, nor you sha'n't now. I shouldn't have a wink of sleep this night if I let you go, and if anything were to happen to you it would be me as 'ud have to answer for it.'

'But I must go; my mother and sister will not know what has become of me.'

'You leave that to me; I tell you again as you can't go. I've been a mother myself, and I haven't had children for nothing. I was just a-goin' to send a little parcel up to my daughter by the coach, and her husband's a-goin' to meet it. She'd left something behind last week when she was with me, and I thought I'd get a

when Mrs Caffyn was not to be seen there, and, if she had to
go to Dorking or Letherhead on business, she always chose
the middle of the day, when the folk were busy at their homes
or in the fields. Poor woman! she was much tried. Half the
people who dealt with her were in her debt, but she could not
press them for her money. During winter-time they were discharged by the score from their farms, but as they were not
sufficiently philosophic, or sufficiently considerate for their
fellows to hang or drown themselves, they were obliged to
consume food, and to wear clothes, for which they tried to pay
by instalments during spring, summer and autumn. Mrs Caffyn
managed to make both ends meet by the help of two or three
pigs, by great economy, and by letting some of her superfluous
rooms. Great Oakhurst was not a show place nor a Spa, but the
Letherhead doctor had once recommended her to a physician in
London, who occasionally sent her a patient who wanted
nothing but rest and fresh air. She also, during the shooting-
season, was often asked to find a bedroom for visitors to The
Towers.

She might have done better had she been on thoroughly good
terms with the parson. She attended church on Sunday morning
with tolerable regularity. She never went inside a dissenting
chapel,* and was not heretical on any definite theological point,
but the rector and she were not friends. She had lived in Surrey
ever since she was a child, but she was not Surrey born. Both
her father and mother came from the north country, and
migrated southwards when she was very young. They were
better educated than the southerners amongst whom they came;
and although their daughter had no schooling beyond what was
obtainable in a Surrey village of that time, she was distinguished
by a certain superiority which she had inherited or acquired
from her parents. She was never subservient to the rector after
the fashion of her neighbours; she never curtsied to him, and if
he passed and nodded she said 'Marnin', sir', in just the same
tone as that in which she said it to the smallest of the Great
Oakhurst farmers. Her church-going was an official duty incum-
bent upon her as the proprietor of the only shop in the parish.

She had nothing to do with church matters except on Sunday, and she even went so far as to neglect to send for the rector when one of her children lay dying. She was attacked for the omission, but she defended herself.

'What was the use when the poor dear was only seven year old? What call was there for him to come to a blessed innocent like that? I did tell him to look in when my husband was took, for I know as before we were married there was something atween him and that gal Sanders. He never would own up to me about it, and I thought as he might to a clergyman, and, if he did, it would ease his mind and make it a bit better for him afterwards; but, Lord! it warn't no use, for he went off and we didn't so much as hear her name, not even when he was a-wandering. I says to myself when the parson left, "What's the good of having you?"'

Mrs Caffyn was a Christian, but she was a disciple of St James rather than of St Paul.* She believed, of course, the doctrines of the Catechism, in the sense that she denied none, and would have assented to all if she had been questioned thereon; but her belief that 'faith, if it hath not works, is dead, being alone', was something very vivid and very practical.

Her estimate, too, of the relative values of the virtues and of the relative sinfulness of sins was original, and the rector therefore told all his parishioners that she was little better than a heathen. The common failings in that part of the country amongst the poor were Saturday-night drunkenness and looseness in the relations between the young men and young women. Mrs Caffyn's indignation never rose to the correct boiling point against these crimes. The rector once ventured to say, as the case was next door to her, –

'It is very sad, is it not, Mrs Caffyn, that Polesden should be so addicted to drink. I hope he did not disturb you last Saturday night. I have given the constable directions to look after the street more closely on Saturday evening, and if Polesden again offends he must be taken up.'

Mrs Caffyn was behind her own counter. She had just served a customer with two ounces of Dutch cheese, and she sat down on her stool. Being rather a heavy woman she always sat down when she was not busy, and she never rose merely to talk.

'Yes, it is sad, sir, and Polesden isn't no particklar friend of mine, but I tell you what's sad too, sir, and that's the way them people are mucked up in that cottage. Why, their living room opens straight on the road, and the wind comes in fit to blow your head off, and when he goes home o' nights, there's them children a-squalling, and he can't bide there and do nothing.'

'I am afraid, though, Mrs Caffyn, there must be something radically wrong with that family. I suppose you know all about the eldest daughter?'

'Yes, sir, I *have* heard it: it wouldn't be Great Oakhurst if I hadn't, but p'r'aps, sir, you've never been upstairs in that house, and yet a house it isn't. There's just two sleeping-rooms, that's all; it's shameful, it isn't decent. Well, that gal, she goes away to service. Maybe, sir, them premises at the farm are also unbeknown to you. In the back kitchen there's a broadish sort of shelf as Jim climbs into o' nights, and it has a rail round it to keep you from a-falling out, and there's a ladder as they draws up in the day as goes straight up from that kitchen to the gal's bedroom door. It's downright disgraceful, and I don't believe the Lord A'mighty would be marciful to neither of *us* if we was tried like that.'

Mrs Caffyn bethought herself of the 'us' and was afraid that even she had gone a little too far; 'leastways, speaking for myself, sir,' she added.

The rector turned rather red, and repented his attempt to enlist Mrs Caffyn.

'If the temptations are so great, Mrs Caffyn, that is all the more reason why those who are liable to them should seek the means which are provided in order that they may be overcome. I believe the Polesdens are very lax attendants at church, and I don't think they ever communicated.'

Mrs Polesden at that moment came in for an ounce of tea, and as Mrs Caffyn rose to weigh it, the rector departed with a stiff 'goodmorning,' made to do duty for both women.

CHAPTER 13

Mrs Caffyn persuaded Madge to go to bed at once, after giving her 'something to comfort her'. In the morning her kind hostess came to her bedside.

'You've got a mother, haven't you – leastways, I know you have, because you wrote to her.'

'Yes.'

'Well, and you lives with her and she looks after you?'

'Yes.'

'And she's fond of you, maybe?'

'Oh, yes.'

'That's a marcy; well then, my dear, you shall go back in the cart to Letherhead, and you'll catch the Darkin coach to London.'

'You have been very good to me; what have I to pay you?'

'Pay? Nothing! why, if I was to let you pay, it would just look as if I'd trapped you here to get something out of you. Pay! no, not a penny.'

'I can afford very well to pay, but if it vexes you I will not offer anything. I don't know how to thank you enough.'

Madge took Mrs Caffyn's hand in hers and pressed it firmly.

'Besides, my dear,' said Mrs Caffyn, smoothing the sheets a little, 'you won't mind my saying it, I expex you are in trouble. There's something on your mind, and I believe as I knows pretty well what it is.'

Madge turned round in the bed so as no longer to face the light; Mrs Caffyn sat between her and the window.

'Look you here, my dear; don't you suppose I meant to say anything to hurt you. The moment I looked on you I was drawed to you like; I couldn't help it. I see'd what was the matter, but I was all the more drawed, and I just wanted you to know as it makes no difference. That's like me; sometimes I'm drawed that way and sometimes t'other way, and it's never no use for me to try to go against it. I ain't a-going to say anything more to you; God-A'mighty, He's above us all; but p'r'aps you may be comin' this way again some day, and then you'll look in.'

Madge turned again to the light, and again caught Mrs Caffyn's hand, but was silent.

The next morning, after Madge's return, Mrs Cork, the landlady, presented herself at the sitting-room door and 'wished to speak with Mrs Hopgood for a minute.'

'Come in, Mrs Cork.'

'Thank you, ma'am, but I prefer as you should come downstairs.'

Mrs Cork was about forty, a widow with no children. She had a face of which it was impossible to recollect, when it had been seen even a dozen times, any feature except the eyes, which were steel-blue, a little bluer than the faceted head of the steel poker in her parlour, but just as hard. She lived in the basement with a maid, much like herself but a little more human. Although the front underground room was furnished Mrs Cork never used it, except on the rarest occasions, and a kind of apron of coloured paper hung over the fireplace nearly all the year. She was a woman of what she called regular habits. No lodger was ever permitted to transgress her rules, or to have meals ten minutes before or ten minutes after the appointed time. She had undoubtedly been married, but who Cork could have been was a marvel. Why he died, and why there were never any children were no marvels. At two o'clock her grate was screwed up to the narrowest possible dimensions, and the ashes, potato peelings, tea leaves and cabbage stalks were thrown on the poor, struggling coals. No meat, by the way, was ever roasted – it was considered wasteful – everything was baked or boiled. After half-past four not a bit of anything that was not cold was allowed till the next morning, and, indeed, from the first of April to the thirty-first of October the fire was raked out the moment tea was over. Mrs Hopgood one night was not very well and Clara wished to give her mother something warm. She rang the bell and asked for hot water. Maria came up and disappeared without a word after receiving the message. Presently she returned.

'Mrs Cork, miss, wishes me to tell you as it was never understood as 'ot water would be required after tea, and she hasn't got any.'

Mrs Hopgood had a fire, although it was not yet the thirty-first of October, for it was very damp and raw. She had with much difficulty induced Mrs Cork to concede this favour (which probably would not have been granted if the coals had not yielded a profit of threepence a scuttleful), and Clara, therefore, asked if she could not have the kettle upstairs. Again Maria disappeared and returned.

'Mrs Cork says, miss, as it's very ill-convenient as the kettle is cleaned up agin tomorrow, and if you can do without it she will be obliged.'

It was of no use to continue the contest, and Clara bethought herself of a little 'Etna' she had in her bedroom. She went to the druggist's, bought some methylated spirit, and obtained what she wanted.

Mrs Cork had one virtue and one weakness. Her virtue was cleanliness, but she persecuted the 'blacks', not because she objected to dirt as dirt, but because it was unauthorised, appeared without permission at irregular hours, and because the glittering polish on varnished paint and red mahogany was a pleasure to her. She liked the dirt, too, in a way, for she enjoyed the exercise of her ill-temper on it and the pursuit of it to destruction. Her weakness was an enormous tom-cat which had a bell round its neck and slept in a basket in the kitchen, the best-behaved and most moral cat in the parish. At half-past nine every evening it was let out into the back-yard and vanished. At ten precisely it was heard to mew and was immediately admitted. Not once in a twelvemonth did that cat prolong its love making after five minutes to ten.

Mrs Hopgood went upstairs to her room, Mrs Cork following and closing the door.

'If you please, ma'am, I wish to give you notice to leave this day week.'

'What is the matter, Mrs Cork?'

'Well, ma'am, for one thing, I didn't know as you'd bring a bird with you.'

It was a pet bird belonging to Madge.

'But what harm does the bird do? It gives no trouble; my daughter attends to it.'

'Yes, ma'am, but it worrits my Joseph – the cat, I mean. I found him the other mornin' on the table eyin' it, and I can't a-bear to see him urritated.'

'I should hardly have thought that a reason for parting with good lodgers.'

Mrs Hopgood had intended to move, as before explained, but she did not wish to go till the three months had expired.

'I don't say as that is everything, but if you wish me to tell you the truth, Miss Madge is not a person as I like to keep in the house. I wish you to know' – Mrs Cork suddenly became excited and venomous – 'that I'm a respectable woman, and have always let my apartments to respectable people, and do you think I should ever let them to respectable people again if it got about as I had had anybody as wasn't respectable? Where was she last night? And do you suppose as me as has been a married woman can't see the condition she's in? I say as you, Mrs Hopgood, ought to be ashamed of yourself for bringing of such a person into a house like mine, and you'll please vacate these premises on the day named.' She did not wait for an answer, but banged the door after her, and went down to her subterranean den.

Mrs Hopgood did not tell her children the true reason for leaving. She merely said that Mrs Cork had been very impertinent, and that they must look out for other rooms. Madge instantly recollected Great Ormond Street, but she did not know the number, and oddly enough she had completely forgotten Mrs Caffyn's name. It was a peculiar name, she had heard it only once, she had not noticed it over the door, and her exhaustion may have had something to do with her loss of memory. She could not therefore write, and Mrs Hopgood determined that she herself would go to Great Oakhurst. She had another reason for her journey. She wished her kind friend there to see that Madge had really a mother who cared for her. She was anxious to confirm Madge's story, and Mrs Caffyn's confidence. Clara desired to go also, but Mrs Hopgood would not leave Madge alone, and the expense of a double fare was considered unnecessary.

When Mrs Hopgood came to Letherhead on her return, the coach was full inside, and she was obliged to ride outside, although the weather was cold and threatening. In about half an hour it began to rain heavily, and by the time she was in Pentonville she was wet through. The next morning she ought to have lain in bed, but she came down at her accustomed hour as Mrs Cork was more than usually disagreeable, and it was settled that they would leave at once if the rooms in Great Ormond Street were available. Clara went there directly after breakfast, and saw Mrs Marshall, who had already received an introductory letter from her mother.

CHAPTER 14

The Marshall family included Marshall and his wife. He was rather a small man, with blackish hair, small lips, and with a nose just a little turned up at the tip. As we have been informed, he was a cabinet-maker. He worked for very good shops, and earned about two pounds a week. He read books, but he did not know their value, and often fancied he had made a great discovery on a bookstall of an author long ago superseded and worthless. He belonged to a mechanic's institute,* and was fond of animal physiology; heard courses of lectures on it at the institute, and had studied two or three elementary handbooks. He found in a second-hand dealer's shop a model, which could be taken to pieces, of the inside of the human body. He had also bought a diagram of a man, showing the circulation, and this he had hung in his bedroom, his mother-in-law objecting most strongly on the ground that its effect on his wife was injurious. He had a notion that the world might be regenerated if men and women were properly instructed in physiological science, and if before marriage they would study their own physical peculiarities, and those of their intended partners. The crossing of peculiarities nevertheless presented difficulties. A man with long legs surely ought to choose a woman with short legs, but if a man who was mathematical married a woman who was mathematical, the result might be a mathematical prodigy. On the other hand the parents of the prodigy might each have corresponding qualities, which, mixed with the mathematical tendency, would completely nullify it. The path of duty therefore was by no means plain. However, Marshall was sure that great cities dwarfed their inhabitants, and as he himself was not so tall as his father, and, moreover, suffered from bad digestion, and had a tendency to 'run to head', he determined to select as his wife a 'daughter of the soil', to use his own phrase, above the average height, with a vigorous constitution and plenty of common sense. She need not be bookish, 'he could supply all that himself'. Accordingly, he married Sarah Caffyn. His mother and Mrs Caffyn had been early friends. He was not mistaken in Sarah. She was certainly robust; she was a shrewd housekeeper, and she never read anything, except now and then a paragraph or two in the weekly newspaper, notwithstanding (for there were no children), time hung rather heavily on her hands. One child had been born, but to Marshall's surprise and disappointment it was a poor, rickety thing, and died before it was a twelvemonth old.

Mrs Marshall was not a very happy woman. Marshall was a great politician and spent many of his evenings away from home at political meetings. He never informed her what he had been doing, and if he had told her, she would neither have understood nor cared anything about it. At Great Oakhurst she heard everything and took an interest in it, and she often wished with all her heart that the subject which occupied Marshall's thoughts was not Chartism* but the draining of that heavy, rush-grown bit of rough pasture that lay at the bottom of the village. He was very good and kind to her, and she never imagined, before marriage, that he ought to be more. She was sure that at Great Oakhurst she would have been quite comfortable with him but somehow, in London, it was different. 'I don't know how it is,' she said one day, 'the sort of husband as does for the country doesn't do for London.'

At Great Oakhurst, where the doors were always open into the yard and the garden, where every house was merely a covered bit of the open space, where people were always in and out, and women never sat down, except to their meals, or to do a little stitching or sewing, it was really not necessary, as Mrs Caffyn observed, that husband and wife should 'hit it so fine'. Mrs Marshall hated all the conveniences of London. She abominated particularly the taps, and longed to be obliged in all weathers to go out to the well and wind up the bucket. She abominated also the dust-bin, for it was a pleasure to be compelled – so at least she thought it now – to walk down to the muck-heap and throw on it what the pig could not eat. Nay, she even missed that corner of the garden against the elder-tree, where the pig-stye was, for 'you could smell the elder-flowers there in the spring-time, and the pig-stye wasn't as bad as the stuffy back room in Great Ormond Street when three or four men were in it'. She did all she could to spend her energy on her cooking and cleaning, but 'there was no satisfaction in it', and she became much depressed, especially after the child died.* This was the main reason why Mrs Caffyn determined to live with her. Marshall was glad she resolved to come. His wife had her full share of the common sense he desired, but the experiment had not altogether succeeded. He knew she was lonely, and he was sorry for her, although he did not see how he could mend matters. He reflected carefully, nothing had happened which was a surprise to him, the relationship was what he had supposed it would be, excepting that the child did not live and its mother was a little miserable. There was nothing he would not do for her, but he really had nothing more to offer her.

Although Mrs Marshall had made up her mind that husbands and wives could not be as contented with one another in the big

city as they would be in a village, a suspicion crossed her mind
one day that, even in London, the relationship might be different
from her own. She was returning from Great Oakhurst after a
visit to her mother. She had stayed there for about a month after
her child's death, and she travelled back to town with a
Letherhead woman, who had married a journeyman tanner,
who formerly worked in the Letherhead tan-yard, and had now
moved to Bermondsey, a horrid hole, worse than Great Ormond
Street. Both Marshall and the tanner were at the Swan with
Two Necks to meet the covered van, and the tanner's wife
jumped out first.

'Hullo, old gal, here you are,' cried the tanner, and clasped
her in his brown, bark-stained arms, giving her, nothing loth,
two or three hearty kisses. They were so much excited at meeting
one another, that they forgot their friends, and marched off
without bidding them goodbye. Mrs Marshall was welcomed in
quieter fashion.

'Ah!' she thought to herself, 'Red Tom,' as the tanner was
called, 'is not used to London ways. They are, perhaps, correct
for London, but Marshall might now and then remember that I
have not been brought up to them.'

To return, however, to the Hopgoods. Before the afternoon
they were in their new quarters, happily for them, for Mrs
Hopgood became worse. On the morrow she was seriously ill,
inflammation of the lungs appeared, and in a week she was
dead. What Clara and Madge suffered cannot be told here.
Whenever anybody whom we love dies, we discover that
although death is commonplace it is terribly original. We may
have thought about it all our lives, but if it comes close to us, it
is quite a new, strange thing to us, for which we are entirely
unprepared. It may, perhaps, not be the bare loss so much as
the strength of the bond which is broken that is the surprise,
and we are debtors in a way to death for revealing something in
us which ordinary life disguises. Long after the first madness of
their grief had passed, Clara and Madge were astonished to find
how dependent they had been on their mother. They were
grown-up women accustomed to act for themselves, but they

felt unsteady, and as if deprived of customary support. The reference to her had been constant, although it was often silent, and they were not conscious of it. A defence from the outside waste desert had been broken down, their mother had always seemed to intervene between them and the world, and now they were exposed and shelterless.

Three parts of Mrs Hopgood's little income was mainly an annuity, and Clara and Madge found that between them they had but seventy-five pounds a year.

CHAPTER 15

Frank could not rest. He wrote again to Clara at Fenmarket; the letter went to Mrs Cork's, and was returned to him. He saw that the Hopgoods had left Fenmarket, and suspecting the reason, he determined at any cost to go home. He accordingly alleged ill-health, a pretext not altogether fictitious, and within a few days after the returned letter reached him he was back at Stoke Newington. He went immediately to the address in Pentonville which he found on the envelope, but was very shortly informed by Mrs Cork that 'she knew nothing whatever about them.' He walked round Myddelton Square, hopeless, for he had no clue whatever.

What had happened to him would scarcely, perhaps, have caused some young men much uneasiness, but with Frank the case was altogether different. There was a chance of discovery, and if his crime should come to light his whole future life would be ruined. He pictured his excommunication, his father's agony, and it was only when it seemed possible that the water might close over the ghastly thing thrown in it, and no ripple reveal what lay underneath, that he was able to breathe again. Immediately he asked himself, however, if he could live with his father and wear a mask, and never betray his dreadful secret. So he wandered homeward in the most miserable of all conditions; he was paralysed by the intricacy of the coil which enveloped and grasped him.

That evening it happened that there was a musical party at his father's house; and, of course, he was expected to assist. It would have suited his mood better if he could have been in his own room, or out in the streets, but absence would have been inconsistent with his disguise, and might have led to betrayal. Consequently he was present, and the gaiety of the company and the excitement of his favourite exercise, brought about for a time forgetfulness of his trouble. Amongst the performers was a distant cousin, Cecilia Morland, a young woman rather tall and fully developed; not strikingly beautiful, but with a lovely reddish-brown tint on her face, indicative of healthy, warm, rich pulsations. She possessed a contralto voice, of a quality like that of a blackbird, and it fell to her and to Frank to sing. She was dressed in a fashion perhaps a little more courtly than was usual in the gatherings at Mr Palmer's house, and Frank, as he stood beside her at the piano, could not restrain his eyes from straying every now and then away from his music to her shoulders, and once nearly lost himself, during a solo which required a little unusual exertion, in watching the movement of a locket and of what was for a moment revealed beneath it. He escorted her amidst applause to a corner of the room, and the two sat down side by side.

'What a long time it is, Frank, since you and I sang that duet together. We have seen nothing of you lately.'

'Of course not; I was in Germany.'

'Yes, but I think you deserted us before then. Do you remember that summer when we were all together at Bonchurch, and the part songs which astonished our neighbours just as it was growing dark? I recollect you and I tried together that very duet for the first time with the old lodging-house piano.'

Frank remembered that evening well.

'You sang better than you did to-night. You did not keep time: what were you dreaming about?'

'How hot the room is! Do you not feel it oppressive? Let us go into the conservatory for a minute.'

The door was behind them and they slipped in and sat down, just inside, and under the orange tree.

'You must not be away so long again. Now mind, we have a musical evening this day fortnight. You will come? Promise; and we must sing that duet again, and sing it properly.'

He did not reply, but he stooped down, plucked a blood-red begonia, and gave it to her.

'That is a pledge. It is very good of you.'

She tried to fasten it in her gown, underneath the locket, but she dropped a little black pin. He went down on his knees to find it; rose, and put the flower in its proper place himself, and his head nearly touched her neck, quite unnecessarily.

'We had better go back now,' she said, 'but mind, I shall keep this flower for a fortnight and a day, and if you make any excuses I shall return it faded and withered.'

'Yes, I will come.'

'Good boy; no apologies like those you sent the last time. No bad throat. Play me false, and there will be a pretty rebuke for you – a dead flower.'

Play me false! It was as if there were some stoppage in a main artery to his brain. *Play me false!* It rang in his ears, and for a moment he saw nothing but the scene at the Hall with Miranda. Fortunately for him, somebody claimed Cecilia, and he slunk back into the greenhouse.

One of Mr Palmer's favourite ballads was *The Three Ravens.** Its pathos unfits it for an ordinary drawing-room, but as the music at Mr Palmer's was not of the common kind, *The Three Ravens* was put on the list for that night.

> *She was dead herself ere evensong time. With a down,*
>   *hey down, hey down,*
> *God send every gentleman*
> *Such hawks, such hounds, and such a leman. With a*
>   *down, hey down, hey down.*

Frank knew well the prayer of that melody, and, as he listened, he painted to himself, in the vividest colours, Madge in a mean room, in a mean lodging, and perhaps dying. The song ceased,

and one for him stood next. He heard voices calling him, but he
passed out into the garden and went down to the further end,
hiding himself behind the shrubs. Presently the inquiry for him
ceased, and he was relieved by hearing an instrumental piece
begin.

Following on that presentation of Madge came self-torture
for his unfaithfulness. He scourged himself into what he considered to be his duty. He recalled with an effort all Madge's
charms, mental and bodily, and he tried to break his heart for
her. He was in anguish because he found that in order to feel as
he ought to feel some effort was necessary; that treason to her
was possible, and because he had looked with such eyes upon
his cousin that evening. He saw himself as something separate
from himself, and although he knew what he saw to be flimsy
and shallow, he could do nothing to deepen it, absolutely
nothing! It was not the betrayal of that thunderstorm which
now tormented him. He could have represented that as a failure
to be surmounted; he could have repented it. It was his own
inner being from which he revolted, from limitations which are
worse than crimes, for who, by taking thought, can add one
cubit to his stature?*

CHAPTER 16

The next morning found Frank once more in Myddelton Square.
He looked up at the house; the windows were all shut, and the
blinds were drawn down. He had half a mind to call again, but
Mrs Cork's manner had been so offensive and repellent that he
desisted. Presently the door opened, and Maria, the maid, came
out to clean the doorsteps. Maria, as we have already said, was
a little more human than her mistress, and having overheard the
conversation between her and Frank at the first interview, had
come to the conclusion that Frank was to be pitied, and she
took a fancy to him. Accordingly, when he passed her, she

looked up and said, – 'Goodmorning'. Frank stopped, and returned her greeting.

'You was here the other day, sir, asking where them Hopgoods had gone.'

'Yes,' said Frank, eagerly, 'do you know what has become of them?'

'I helped the cabman with the boxes, and I heard Mrs Hopgood say "Great Ormond Street", but I have forgotten the number.'

'Thank you very much.'

Frank gave the astonished and grateful Maria half-a-crown, and went off to Great Ormond Street at once. He paced up and down the street half a dozen times, hoping he might recognise in a window some ornament from Fenmarket, or perhaps that he might be able to distinguish a piece of Fenmarket furniture, but his search was in vain, for the two girls had taken furnished rooms at the back of the house. His quest was not renewed that week. What was there to be gained by going over the ground again? Perhaps they might have found the lodgings unsuitable and have moved elsewhere. At church on Sunday he met his cousin Cecilia, who reminded him of his promise.

'See,' she said, 'here is the begonia. I put it in my prayer-book in order to preserve it when I could keep it in water no longer, and it has stained the leaf, and spoilt the Athanasian Creed.* You will have it sent to you if you are faithless. Reflect on your emotions, sir, when you receive a dead flower, and you have the bitter consciousness also that you have damaged my creed without any recompense.'

It was impossible not to protest that he had no thought of breaking his engagement, although, to tell the truth, he had wished once or twice he could find some way out of it. He walked with her down the churchyard path to her carriage, assisted her into it, saluted her father and mother, and then went home with his own people.

The evening came, he sang with Cecilia, and it was observed, and he himself observed it, how completely their voices harmonised. He was not without a competitor, a handsome young baritone, who was much commended. When he came to the end of his performance everybody said what a pity it was that the following duet could not also be given, a duet which Cecilia knew perfectly well. She was very much pressed to take her part with him, but she steadily refused, on the ground that she had not practised it, that she had already sung once, and that she was engaged to sing once more with her cousin. Frank was sitting next to her, and she added, so as to be heard by him alone, 'He is no particular favourite of mine.'

There was no direct implication that Frank was a favourite, but an inference was possible, and at least it was clear that she preferred to reserve herself for him. Cecilia's gifts, her fortune, and her gay, happy face had made many a young fellow restless, and had brought several proposals, none of which had been accepted. All this Frank knew, and how could he repress something more than satisfaction when he thought that perhaps he might have been the reason why nobody as yet had been able to win her. She always called him Frank, for although they were not first cousins, they were cousins. He generally called her Cecilia, but she was Cissy in her own house. He was hardly close enough to venture upon the more familiar nickname, but tonight, as they rose to go to the piano, he said, and the baritone sat next to her, –

'Now, *Cissy*, once more.'

She looked at him with just a little start of surprise, and a smile spread itself over her face. After they had finished, and she never sang better, the baritone noticed that she seemed indisposed to return to her former place, and she retired with Frank to the opposite corner of the room.

'I wonder,' she said, 'if being happy in a thing is a sign of being born to do it. If it is, I am born to be a musician.'

'I should say it is; if two people are quite happy in one another's company, it is as a sign they were born for one another.'

'Yes, if they are sure they are happy. It is easier for me to be sure that I am happier with a thing than with a person.'

'Do you think so? Why?'

'There is the uncertainty whether the person is happy with me. I cannot be altogether happy with anybody unless I know I make him happy.'

'What kind of person is he with whom you *could* be without making him happy?'

The baritone rose to the upper F with a clash of chords on the piano, and the company broke up. Frank went home with but one thought in his head – the thought of Cecilia.

His bedroom faced the south-west, its windows were open, and when he entered, the wind, which was gradually rising, struck him on the face and nearly forced the door out of his hand; the fire in his blood was quenched, and the image of Cecilia receded. He looked out, and saw reflected on the low clouds the dull glare of the distant city. Just over there was Great Ormond Street, and underneath that dim, red light, like the light of a great house burning, was Madge Hopgood. He lay down, turning over from side to side in the vain hope that by change of position he might sleep. After about an hour's feverish tossing, he just lost himself, but not in that oblivion which slumber usually brought him. He was so far awake that he saw what was around him, and yet, he was so far released from the control of his reason that he did not recognise what he saw, and it became part of a new scene created by his delirium. The full moon, clearing away the clouds as she moved upwards, had now passed round to the south, and just caught the white window-curtain farthest from him. He half-opened his eyes, his mad dream still clung to him, and there was the dead Madge before him, pale in death, and holding a child in her arms! He distinctly heard himself scream as he started up in affright; he could not tell where he was; the spectre faded and the furniture and hangings transformed themselves into their familiar reality. He could not lie down again, and rose and dressed himself. He was not the man to believe that the ghost could be a revelation or a prophecy, but, nevertheless, he was once more overcome with fear, a vague dread partly justifiable by the fact of Madge, by the fact that his father might soon know what had happened, that others also might know, Cecilia for example, but partly also a fear going beyond all the facts, and not to be accounted for by them, a strange, horrible trembling such as men feel in earthquakes when the solid rock shakes, on which everything rests.

CHAPTER 17

When Frank came downstairs to breakfast the conversation turned upon his return to Germany. He did not object to going, although it can hardly be said that he willed to go. He was in that perilous condition in which the comparison of reasons is impossible, and the course taken depends upon some chance impulse of the moment, and is a mere drift. He could not leave, however, in complete ignorance of Madge, and with no certainty as to her future. He resolved therefore to make one more effort to discover the house. That was all which he determined to do. What was to happen when he had found it, he did not know. He was driven to do something, which could not be of any importance, save for what must follow, but he was unable to bring himself even to consider what was to follow. He knew that at Fenmarket one or other of the sisters went out soon after breakfast to make provision for the day, and perhaps, if they kept up this custom, he might be successful in his search. He accordingly stationed himself in Great Ormond Street at about half-past nine, and kept watch from the Lamb's Conduit Street end, shifting his position as well as he could, in order to escape notice. He had not been there half an hour when he saw a door open, and Madge came out and went westwards. She turned down Devonshire Street as if on her way to Holborn. He instantly ran back to Theobalds Road, and when he came to the corner of Devonshire Street she was about ten yards from him, and he faced her. She stopped irresolutely, as if she had a mind to return, but as he approached her, and she found she was recognised, she came towards him.

'Madge, Madge,' he cried, 'I want to speak to you. I must speak with you.'

'Better not; let me go.'

'I say I *must* speak to you.'

'We cannot talk here; let me go.'

'I must! I must! come with me.'

She pitied him, and although she did not consent she did not refuse. He called a cab, and in ten minutes, not a word having been spoken during those ten minutes, they were at St Paul's. The morning service had just begun, and they sat down in a corner far away from the worshippers.

'Oh, Madge,' he began, 'I implore you to take me back. I love you. I do love you, and – and – I cannot leave you.'

She was side by side with the father of her child about to be born. He was not and could not be as another man to her, and for the moment there was the danger lest she should mistake this secret bond for love. The thought of what had passed between them, and of the child, his and hers, almost overpowered her.

'I cannot,' he repeated. 'I *ought* not. What will become of me?'

She felt herself stronger; he was excited, but his excitement was not contagious. The string vibrated, and the note was resonant, but it was not a note which synchronised with her, and it did not stir her to respond. He might love her, he was sincere enough to sacrifice himself for her, and to remain faithful to her, but the voice was not altogether that of his own true self. Partly, at least, it was the voice of what he considered to be duty, of superstition and alarm. She was silent.

'Madge,' he continued, 'ought you to refuse? You have some love for me. Is it not greater than the love which thousands feel for one another. Will you blast your future and mine, and, perhaps, that of someone besides, who may be very dear to you? *Ought* you not, I say, to listen?'

The service had come to an end, the organist was playing a voluntary, rather longer than usual, and the congregation was leaving, some of them passing near Madge and Frank, and

casting idle glances on the young couple who had evidently
come neither to pray nor to admire the architecture. Madge
recognised the well-known St Ann's fugue,* and, strange to say,
even at such a moment it took entire possession of her; the
golden ladder was let down and celestial visitors descended.
When the music ceased she spoke.

'It would be a crime.'

'A crime, but I – ' She stopped him.

'I know what you are going to say. I know what is the crime
to the world; but it would have been a crime, perhaps a worse
crime, if a ceremony had been performed beforehand by a priest,
and the worst of crimes would be that ceremony now. I must
go.' She rose and began to move towards the door.

He walked silently by her side till they were in St Paul's
churchyard, when she took him by the hand, pressed it affection-
ately and suddenly turned into one of the courts that lead
towards Paternoster Row. He did not follow her, something
repelled him, and when he reached home it crossed his mind
that marriage, after such delay, would be a poor recompense, as
he could not thereby conceal her disgrace.

CHAPTER 18

It was clear that these two women could not live in London on
seventy-five pounds a year, most certainly not with the prospect
before them, and Clara cast about for something to do. Marshall
had a brother-in-law, a certain Baruch Cohen, a mathematical
instrument maker* in Clerkenwell, and to him Marshall acci-
dentally one day talked about Clara, and said that she desired
an occupation. Cohen himself could not give Clara any work,
but he knew a second-hand bookseller, an old man who kept a
shop in Holborn, who wanted a clerk, and Clara thus found
herself earning another pound a week. With this addition she
and her sister could manage to pay their way and provide what

Madge would want. The hours were long, the duties irksome and wearisome, and, worst of all, the conditions under which they were performed, were not only as bad as they could be, but their badness was of a kind to which Clara had never been accustomed, so that she felt every particle of it in its full force. The windows of the shop were, of course, full of books, and the walls were lined with them. In the middle of the shop also was a range of shelves, and books were stacked on the floor, so that the place looked like a huge cubical block of them through which passages had been bored. At the back the shop became contracted in width to about eight feet, and consequently the central shelves were not continued there, but just where they ended, and overshadowed by them were a little desk and a stool. All round the desk more books were piled, and some manœuvring was necessary in order to sit down. This was Clara's station. Occasionally, on a brilliant, a very brilliant day in summer, she could write without gas, but, perhaps, there were not a dozen such days in the year. By twisting herself sideways she could just catch a glimpse of a narrow line of sky over some heavy theology which was not likely to be disturbed, and was therefore put at the top of the window, and once when somebody bought the *Calvin Joann. Opera Omnia, 9 vol. folio, Amst.** 1671 – it was very clear that afternoon – she actually descried towards seven o'clock a blessed star exactly in the middle of the gap the Calvin had left.

The darkness was very depressing, and poor Clara often shut her eyes as she bent over her day-book and ledger, and thought of the Fenmarket flats where the sun could be seen bisected by the horizon at sun-rising and sun-setting, and where even the southern Antares* shone with diamond glitter close to the ground during summer nights. She tried to reason with herself during the dreadful smoke fogs; she said to herself that they were only half-a-mile thick, and she carried herself up in imagination and beheld the unclouded azure, the filthy smother lying all beneath her, but her dream did not continue, and reality was too strong for her. Worse, perhaps, than the eternal gloom was the dirt. She was naturally fastidious, and as her skin was

thin and sensitive, dust was physically a discomfort. Even at
Fenmarket she was continually washing her hands and face,
and, indeed, a wash was more necessary to her after a walk than
food or drink. It was impossible to remain clean in Holborn for
five minutes; everything she touched was foul with grime; her
collar and cuffs were black with it when she went home to her
dinner, and it was not like the honest, blowing road-sand of
Fenmarket highways, but a loathsome composition of everything disgusting which could be produced by millions of human
beings and animals packed together in soot. It was a real misery
to her and made her almost ill. However, she managed to set up
for herself a little lavatory in the basement, and whenever she
had a minute at her command, she descended and enjoyed the
luxury of a cool, dripping sponge and a piece of yellow soap.
The smuts began to gather again the moment she went upstairs,
but she strove to arm herself with a little philosophy against
them. 'What is there in life,' she moralised, smiling at her
sermonising, 'which once won is for ever won? It is always being
won and always being lost.' Her master, fortunately, was one of
the kindest of men, an old gentleman of about sixty-five, who
wore a white necktie, clean every morning. He was really a
*gentle*man in the true sense of that much misused word, and not
a mere *trades*man; that is to say, he loved his business, not
altogether for the money it brought him, but as an art. He was
known far and wide, and literary people were glad to gossip
with him. He never pushed his wares, and he hated to sell them
to anybody who did not know their value. He amused Clara
one afternoon when a carriage stopped at the door, and a lady
inquired if he had a Manning and Bray's *History of Surrey*.*
Yes, he had a copy, and he pointed to the three handsome, tall
folios.

'What is the price?'

'Twelve pounds ten.'

'I think I will have them.'

'Madam, you will pardon me, but, if I were you, I would not.
I think something much cheaper will suit you better. If you will
allow me, I will look out for you and will report in a few days.'

'Oh! very well,' and she departed.

'The wife of a brassfounder,' he said to Clara; 'made a lot of money, and now he has bought a house at Dulwich and is setting up a library. Somebody has told him that he ought to have a county history, and that Manning and Bray is the book. Manning and Bray! What he wants is a Dulwich and Denmark Hill Directory.* No, no,' and he took down one of the big volumes, blew the dust off the top edges and looked at the old book-plate inside, 'you won't go there if I can help it.' He took a fancy to Clara when he found she loved literature, although what she read was out of his department altogether, and his perfectly human behaviour to her prevented that sense of exile and loneliness which is so horrible to many a poor creature who comes up to London to begin therein the struggle for existence. She read and meditated a good deal in the shop, but not to much profit, for she was continually interrupted, and the thought of her sister intruded itself perpetually.

Madge seldom or never spoke of her separation from Frank, but one night, when she was somewhat less reserved than usual, Clara ventured to ask her if she had heard from him since they parted.

'I met him once.'

'Madge, do you mean that he found out where we are living, and that he came to see you?'

'No, it was just round the corner as I was going towards Holborn.'

'Nothing could have brought him here but yourself,' said Clara, slowly.

'Clara, you doubt?'

'No, no! I doubt you? Never!'

'But you hesitate; you reflect. Speak out.'

'God forbid I should utter a word which would induce you to disbelieve what you know to be right. It is much more important to believe earnestly that something is morally right than that it should be really right, and he who attempts to displace a belief runs a certain risk, because he is not sure that what he substitutes can be held with equal force. Besides, each person's belief, or proposed course of action, is a part of himself, and if he be diverted from it and takes up with that which is not himself, the unity of his nature is impaired, and he loses himself.'

'Which is as much as to say that the prophet is to break no idols.'

'You know I do not mean that, and you know, too, how incapable I am of defending myself in argument. I never can stand up for anything I say. I can now and then say something, but, when I have said it, I run away.'

'My dearest Clara,' Madge put her arm over her sister's shoulder as they sat side by side, 'do not run away now; tell me just what you think of me.'

Clara was silent for a minute.

'I have sometimes wondered whether you have not demanded a little too much of yourself and Frank. It is always a question of how much. There is no human truth which is altogether true, no love which is altogether perfect. You may possibly have neglected virtue or devotion such as you could not find elsewhere, overlooking it because some failing, or the lack of sympathy on some unimportant point, may at the moment have been prominent. Frank loved you, Madge.'

Madge did not reply; she withdrew her arm from her sister's neck, threw herself back in her chair and closed her eyes. She saw again the Fenmarket roads, that summer evening, and she felt once more Frank's burning caresses. She thought of him as he left St Paul's, perhaps broken-hearted. Stronger than every other motive to return to him, and stronger than ever, was the movement towards him of that which belonged to him.

At last she cried out, literally cried, with a vehemence which startled and terrified Clara, –

'Clara, Clara, you know not what you do! For God's sake forbear!' She was again silent, and then she turned round hurriedly, hid her face, and sobbed piteously. It lasted, however, but for a minute; she rose, wiped her eyes, went to the window, came back again, and said, –

'It is beginning to snow.'

The iron pillar bolted to the solid rock had quivered and

resounded under the blow, but its vibrations were nothing more than those of the rigid metal; the base was unshaken and, except for an instant, the column had not been deflected a hair's-breadth.

CHAPTER 19

Mr Cohen, who had obtained the situation indirectly for Clara, thought nothing more about it until, one day, he went to the shop, and he then recollected his recommendation, which had been given solely in faith, for he had never seen the young woman, and had trusted entirely to Marshall. He found her at her dark desk, and as he approached her, she hastily put a mark in a book and closed it.

'Have you sold a little volume called *After Office Hours* by a man named Robinson?'*

'I did not know we had it. I have never seen it.'

'I do not wonder, but I saw it here about six months ago; it was up there,' pointing to a top shelf. Clara was about to mount the ladder, but he stopped her, and found what he wanted. Some of the leaves were torn.

'We can repair those for you; in about a couple of days it shall be ready.'

He lingered a little, and at that moment another customer entered. Clara went forward to speak to him, and Cohen was able to see that it was the *Heroes and Hero Worship** she had been studying, a course of lectures which had been given by a Mr Carlyle, of whom Cohen knew something. As the customer showed no signs of departing, Cohen left, saying he would call again.

Before sending Robinson's *After Office Hours* to the binder, Clara looked at it. It was made up of short essays, about twenty altogether, bound in dark-green cloth, lettered at the side, and published in 1841. They were upon the oddest subjects: such as,

Ought Children to learn Rules before Reasons? The Higher Mathematics and Materialism. Ought We to tell Those Whom We love what We think about Them? Deductive Reasoning in Politics. What Troubles ought We to Make Known and What ought We to Keep Secret: Courage as a Science and an Art.

Clara did not read any one essay through, she had no time, but she was somewhat struck with a few sentences which caught her eye; for example –

'A mere dream, a vague hope, ought in some cases to be more potent than a certainty in regulating our action. The faintest vision of God should be more determinative than the grossest earthly assurance.'

'I knew a case in which a man had to encounter three successive trials of all the courage and inventive faculty in him. Failure in one would have been ruin. The odds against him in each trial were desperate, and against ultimate victory were overwhelming. Nevertheless, he made the attempt, and was triumphant, by the narrowest margin, in every struggle. That which is of most value to us is often obtained in defiance of the laws of probability.'

'What is precious in Quakerism* is not so much the doctrine of the Divine voice as that of the preliminary stillness, the closure against other voices and the reduction of the mind to a condition in which it can *listen*, in which it can discern the merest whisper, inaudible when the world, or interest, or passion, are permitted to speak.'

'The acutest syllogiser can never develop the actual consequences of any system of policy, or, indeed, of any change in human relationship, man being so infinitely complex, and the interaction of human forces so incalculable.'

'Many of our speculative difficulties arise from the unauthorised conception of an *omnipotent* God, a conception entirely of our own creation, and one which, if we look at it closely, has no meaning. It is because God *could* have done otherwise, and did not, that we are confounded. It may be distressing to think that God cannot do any better, but it is not so distressing as to believe that He might have done better had He so willed.'

Although these passages were disconnected, each of them seemed to Clara to be written in a measure for herself, and her curiosity was excited about the author. Perhaps the man who called would say something about him.

Baruch Cohen was now a little over forty. He was half a Jew, for his father was a Jew and his mother a Gentile. The father had broken with Judaism, but had not been converted to any Christian church or sect. He was a diamond-cutter, originally from Holland, came over to England and married the daughter of a mathematical instrument maker, at whose house he lodged in Clerkenwell. The son was apprenticed to his maternal grandfather's trade, became very skilful at it, worked at it himself, employed a man and a boy, and supplied London shops, which sold his instruments at about three times the price he obtained for them. Baruch, when he was very young, married Marshall's elder sister, but she died at the birth of her first child and he had been a widower now for nineteen years. He had often thought of taking another wife, and had seen, during these nineteen years, two or three women with whom he had imagined himself to be really in love, and to whom he had been on the verge of making proposals, but in each case he had hung back, and when he found that a second and a third had awakened the same ardour for a time as the first, he distrusted its genuineness. He was now, too, at a time of life when a man has to make the unpleasant discovery that he is beginning to lose the right to expect what he still eagerly desires, and that he must beware of being ridiculous. It is indeed a very unpleasant discovery. If he has done anything well which was worth doing, or has made himself a name, he may be treated by women with respect or adulation, but any passable boy of twenty is really more interesting to them, and, unhappily, there is perhaps so much of the man left in him that he would rather see the eyes of a girl melt when she looked at him than be adored by all the drawing-rooms in London as the author of the greatest poem since *Paradise Lost*,* or as the conqueror of half a continent. Baruch's life during the last nineteen years had been such that he was still young, and he desired more than ever, because not so blindly as he desired it when he was a youth, the tender, intimate sympathy of a woman's love. It was singular that, during all those nineteen years, he should not once have been overcome. It seemed to him as if he had been held back, not by himself, but by some external power, which refused to give any reasons for so doing. There was now less chance of yielding than ever; he was reserved and self-respectful, and his manner towards women distinctly announced to them that he knew what he was and that he had no claims whatever upon them. He was something of a philosopher, too; he accepted, therefore, as well as he could, without complaint, the inevitable order of nature, and he tried to acquire, although often he failed, that blessed art of taking up lightly and even with a smile whatever he was compelled to handle. 'It is possible,' he said once, 'to consider death too seriously.' He was naturally more than half a Jew; his features were Jewish, his thinking was Jewish, and he believed after a fashion in the Jewish sacred books, or, at any rate, read them continuously, although he had added to his armoury defensive weapons of another type. In nothing was he more Jewish than in a tendency to dwell upon the One, or what he called God, clinging still to the expression of his forefathers although departing so widely from them. In his ethics and system of life, as well as in his religion, there was the same intolerance of a multiplicity which was not reducible to unity. He seldom explained his theory, but everybody who knew him recognised the difference which it wrought between him and other men. There was a certain concord in everything he said and did, as if it were directed by some enthroned but secret principle.

He had encountered no particular trouble since his wife's death, but his life had been unhappy. He had no friends, much as he longed for friendship, and he could not give any reasons for his failure. He saw other persons more successful, but he remained solitary. Their needs were not so great as his, for it is not those who have the least but those who have the most to give who most want sympathy. He had often made advances; people had called on him and had appeared interested in him, but they had dropped away. The cause was chiefly to be found in his nationality. The ordinary Englishman disliked him simply as a Jew, and the better sort were repelled by a lack of geniality and by his inability to manifest a healthy interest in personal details. Partly also the cause was that those who care to speak about what is nearest to them are very rare, and most persons find conversation easy in proportion to the remoteness of its topics from them. Whatever the reasons may have been, Baruch now, no matter what the pressure from within might be, generally kept himself to himself. It was a mistake and he ought not to have retreated so far upon repulse. A word will sometimes, when least expected, unlock a heart, a soul is gained for ever, and at once there is much more than a recompense for the indifference of years.

After the death of his wife, Baruch's affection spent itself upon his son Benjamin, whom he had apprenticed to a firm of optical instrument makers in York. The boy was not very much like his father. He was indifferent to that religion by which his father lived, but he inherited an aptitude for mathematics, which was very necessary in his trade. Benjamin also possessed his father's rectitude, trusted him, and looked to him for advice to such a degree that even Baruch, at last, thought it would be better to send him away from home in order that he might become a little more self-reliant and independent. It was the sorest of trials to part with him, and, for some time after he left, Baruch's loneliness was intolerable. It was, however, relieved by a visit to York perhaps once in four or five months, for whenever business could be alleged as an excuse for going north, he managed, as he said, 'to take York on his way.'

The day after he met Clara he started for Birmingham, and although York was certainly not 'on his way,' he pushed forward to the city and reached it on a Saturday evening. He was to spend Sunday there, and on Sunday morning he proposed that they should hear the cathedral service, and go for a walk in the afternoon. To this suggestion Benjamin partially assented. He wished to go to the cathedral in the morning, but thought his father had better rest after dinner. Baruch somewhat resented the insinuation of possible fatigue consequent on advancing years.

'What do you mean?' he said; 'you know well enough I enjoy a walk in the afternoon; besides, I shall not see much of you, and do not want to lose what little time I have.'

About three, therefore, they started, and presently a girl met them, who was introduced simply as 'Miss Masters'.

'We are going to your side of the water,' said the son; 'you may as well cross with us.'

They came to a point where a boat was moored, and a man was in it. There was no regular ferry, but on Sundays he earned a trifle by taking people to the opposite meadow, and thus enabling them to vary their return journey to the city. When they were about two-thirds of the way over, Benjamin observed that if they stood up they could see the Minster. They all three rose, and without an instant's warning – they could not tell afterwards how it happened – the boat half capsized, and they were in eight or nine feet of water. Baruch could not swim and went down at once, but on coming up close to the gunwale he caught at it and held fast. Looking round, he saw that Benjamin, who could swim well, had made for Miss Masters, and, having caught her by the back of the neck, was taking her ashore. The boatman, who could also swim, called out to Baruch to hold on, gave the boat three or four vigorous strokes from the stern, and Baruch felt the ground under his feet. The boatman's little cottage was not far off, and, when the party reached it, Benjamin earnestly desired Miss Masters to take off her wet clothes and occupy the bed which was offered her. He himself would run home – it was not half-a-mile – and, after having changed, would go to her house and send her sister with what was wanted. He was just off when it suddenly struck him that his father might need some attention.

'Oh, father – ' he began, but the boatman's wife interposed.

'He can't be left like that, and he can't go home; he'll catch his death o' cold, and there isn't but one more bed in the house, and that isn't quite fit to put a gentleman in. Howsomever, he must turn in there, and my husband, he can go into the back-kitchen and rub himself down. You won't do yourself no good, Mr Cohen,' addressing the son, whom she knew, 'by going back; you'd better stay here and get into bed with your father.'

In a few minutes the boatman would have gone on the errand, but Benjamin could not lose the opportunity of sacrificing himself for Miss Masters. He rushed off, and in threequarters of an hour had returned with the sister. Having learned, after anxious inquiry, that Miss Masters, so far as could be discovered, had not caught a chill, he went to his father.

'Well, father, I hope you are none the worse for the ducking,' he said gaily. 'The next time you come to York you'd better bring another suit of clothes with you.'

Baruch turned round uneasily and did not answer immediately. He had had a narrow escape from drowning.

'Nothing of much consequence. Is your friend all right?'

'Oh, yes; I was anxious about her, for she is not very strong, but I do not think she will come to much harm. I made them light a fire in her room.'

'Are they drying my clothes?'

'I'll go and see.'

He went away and encountered the elder Miss Masters, who told him that her sister, feeling no ill effects from the plunge, had determined to go home at once, and in fact was nearly ready. Benjamin waited, and presently she came downstairs, smiling.

'Nothing the matter. I owe it to you, however, that I am not now in another world.'

Benjamin was in an ecstasy, and considered himself bound to accompany her to her door.

Meanwhile, Baruch lay upstairs alone in no very happy temper. He heard the conversation below, and knew that his son had gone. In all genuine love there is something of ferocious selfishness. The perfectly divine nature knows how to keep it in check, and is even capable – supposing it to be a woman's nature – of contentment if the loved one is happy, no matter with what or with whom; but the nature only a little less than divine cannot, without pain, endure the thought that it no longer owns privately and exclusively that which it loves, even when it loves a child, and Baruch was particularly excusable, considering his solitude. Nevertheless, he had learned a little wisdom, and, what was of much greater importance, had learned how to use it when he needed it. It had been forced upon him; it was an adjustment to circumstances, the wisest wisdom. It was not something without any particular connection with him; it was rather the external protection built up from within to shield him where he was vulnerable; it was the answer to questions which had been put to *him*, and not to those which had been put to other people. So it came to pass that, when he said bitterly to himself that, if he had at that moment being lying dead at the bottom of the river, Benjamin would have found consolation very near at hand, he was able to reflect upon the folly of self-laceration, and to rebuke himself for a complaint against what was simply the order of Nature, and not a personal failure. His self-conquest, however, was not very permanent. When he left York the next morning, he fancied his son was not particularly grieved, and he was passive under the thought that an epoch in his life had come, that the milestones now began to show the distance to the place to which he travelled, and, still worse, that the boy who had been so close to him, and upon whom he had so much depended, had gone from him.

There is no remedy for our troubles which is uniformly and progressively efficacious. All that we have a right to expect from our religion is that gradually, very gradually, it will assist us to a real victory. After each apparent defeat, if we are bravely in earnest, we gain something on our former position. Baruch was two days on his journey back to town, and as he came nearer home, he recovered himself a little. Suddenly he remembered the bookshop and the book for which he had to call, and that he had intended to ask Marshall something about the bookseller's new assistant.

CHAPTER 20

Madge was a puzzle to Mrs Caffyn. Mrs Caffyn loved her, and when she was ill had behaved like a mother to her. The newly-born child, a healthy girl, was treated by Mrs Caffyn as if it were her own grand-daughter, and many little luxuries were bought which never appeared in Mrs Marshall's weekly bill. Naturally, Mrs Caffyn's affection moved a response from Madge, and Mrs Caffyn by degrees heard the greater part of her history; but why she had separated herself from her lover without any apparent reason remained a mystery, and all the greater was the mystery because Mrs Caffyn believed that there were no other facts to be known than those she knew. She longed to bring about a reconciliation. It was dreadful to her that Madge should be condemned to poverty, and that her infant should be fatherless, although there was a gentleman waiting to take them both and make them happy.

'The hair won't be dark like yours, my love,' she said one afternoon, soon after Madge had come downstairs and was lying on the sofa. 'The hair do darken a lot, but hers will never be black. It's my opinion as it'll be fair.'

Madge did not speak, and Mrs Caffyn, who was sitting at the head of the couch, put her work and her spectacles on the table. It was growing dusk; she took Madge's hand, which hung down by her side, and gently lifted it up. Such a delicate hand, Mrs Caffyn thought. She was proud that she had for a friend the owner of such a hand, who behaved to her as an equal. It was delightful to be kissed – no mere formal salutations – by a lady fit to go into the finest drawing-room in London, but it was a greater delight that Madge's talk suited her better than any she had heard at Great Oakhurst. It was natural she should rejoice when she discovered, unconsciously that she had a soul, to which the speech of the stars, though somewhat strange, was not an utterly foreign tongue.

She retained her hold on Madge's hand.

'May be,' she continued, 'it'll be like its father's. In our family all the gals take after the father, and all the boys after the mother. I suppose as *he* has lightish hair?'

Still Madge said nothing.

'It isn't easy to believe as the father of that blessed dear could have been a bad lot. I'm sure he isn't, and yet there's that Polesden gal at the farm, she as went wrong with Jim, a great ugly brute, and she herself warnt up to much, well, as I say, her child was the delicatest little angel as I ever saw. It's my belief as God-a-mighty mixes Hisself up in it more nor we think. But there *was* nothing amiss with him, was there, my sweet?'

Mrs Caffyn inclined her head towards Madge.

'Oh, no! Nothing, nothing.'

'Don't you think, my dear, if there's nothing atwixt you, as it was a flyin' in the face of Providence to turn him off? You were reglarly engaged to him, and I have heard you say he was very fond of you. I suppose there were some high words about something, and a kind of a quarrel like, and so you parted, but that's nothing. It might all be made up now, and it ought to be made up. What was it about?'

'There was no quarrel.'

'Well, of course, if you don't like to say anything more to me, I won't ask you. I don't want to hear any secrets as I shouldn't hear. I speak only because I can't abear to see you here when I believe as everything might be put right, and you might have a house of your own, and a good husband, and be happy for the rest of your days. It isn't too late for that now. I know what I know, and as how he'd marry you at once.'

'Oh, my dear Mrs Caffyn, I have no secret from you, who have been so good to me; I can only say I could not love him – not as I ought.'

'If you can't love a man, that is to say if you can't *abear* him, it's wrong to have him, but if there's a child that does make a difference, for one has to think of the child and of being respectable. There's something in being respectable; although, for that matter, I've see'd respectable people at Great Oakhurst

as were ten times worse than those as aren't. Still, a-speaking
for myself, I'd put up with a goodish bit to marry the man
whose child wor mine.'

'For myself I could, but it wouldn't be just to him.'

'I don't see what you mean.'

'I mean that I could sacrifice myself if I believed it to be my
duty, but I should wrong him cruelly if I were to accept him and
did not love him with all my heart.'

'My dear, you take my word for it, he isn't so particklar as
you are. A man isn't so particklar as a woman. He goes about
his work, and has all sorts of things in his head, and if a woman
makes him comfortable when he comes home, he's all right. I
won't say as one woman is much the same as another to a man
– leastways to all men – but still they are not particklar. Maybe,
though, it isn't quite the same with gentlefolk like yourself, –
but there's that blessed baby a-cryin'.'

Mrs Caffyn hastened upstairs, leaving Madge to her reflections. Once more the old dialectic reappeared. 'After all,' she
thought, 'it is, as Clara said, a question of degree. There are not
a thousand husbands and wives in this great city whose relationship comes near perfection. If I felt aversion my course would
be clear, but there is no aversion; on the contrary, our affection
for one another is sufficient for a decent household and decent
existence undisturbed by catastrophes. No brighter sunlight is
obtained by others far better than myself. Ought I to expect a
refinement of relationship to which I have no right? Our claims
are always beyond our deserts, and we are disappointed if our
poor, mean, defective natures do not obtain the homage which
belongs to those of ethereal texture. It will be a life with no
enthusiasms nor romance, perhaps, but it will be tolerable, and
what may be called happy, and my child will be protected and
educated. My child! what is there which I ought to put in the
balance against her? If our sympathy is not complete, I have my
own little oratory: I can keep the candles alight, close the door,
and worship there alone.'

So she mused, and her foes again ranged themselves over
against her. There was nothing to support her but something

veiled, which would not altogether disclose or explain itself. Nevertheless, in a few minutes, her enemies had vanished, like a mist before a sudden wind, and she was once more victorious. Precious and rare are those divine souls, to whom that which is aerial is substantial, the only true substance; those for whom a pale vision possesses an authority they are forced unconditionally to obey.

CHAPTER 21

Mrs Caffyn was unhappy, and made up her mind that she would talk to Frank herself. She had learned enough about him from the two sisters, especially from Clara, to make her believe that, with a very little management, she could bring him back to Madge. The difficulty was to see him without his father's knowledge. At last she determined to write to him, and she made her son-in-law address the envelope and mark it private. This is what she said: –

> Dear Sir, – Although unbeknown to you, I take the liberty of telling you as M. H. is alivin' here with me, and somebody else as I think you ought to see, but perhaps I'd better have a word or two with you myself, if not quite ill-convenient to you, and maybe you'll be kind enough to say how that's to be done to your obedient, humble servant,
>
> Mrs Caffyn

She thought this very diplomatic, inasmuch as nobody but Frank could possibly suspect what the letter meant. It went to Stoke Newington, but, alas! he was in Germany, and poor Mrs Caffyn had to wait a week before she received a reply. Frank of course understood it. Although he had thought about Madge continually, he had become calmer. He saw, it is true, that there was no stability in his position, and that he could not possibly remain where he was. Had Madge been the commonest of the common, and his relationship to her the commonest of the common, he could not permit her to cast herself loose from him for ever and take upon herself the whole burden of his misdeed. But he did not know what to do, and, as successive considerations and reconsiderations ended in nothing, and the distractions of a foreign country were so numerous, Madge had for a time been put aside, like a huge bill which we cannot pay, and which staggers us. We therefore docket it, and hide it in the desk, and we imagine we have done something. Once again, however, the flame leapt up out of the ashes, vivid as ever. Once again the thought that he had been so close to Madge, and that she had yielded to him, touched him with peculiar tenderness, and it seemed impossible to part himself from her. To a man with any of the nobler qualities of man it is not only a sense of honour which binds him to a woman who has given him all she has to give. Separation seems unnatural, monstrous, a divorce from himself; it is not she alone, but it is himself whom he abandons. Frank's duty, too, pointed imperiously to the path he ought to take, duty to the child as well as to the mother. He determined to go home, secretly; Mrs Caffyn would not have written if she had not seen good reason for believing that Madge still belonged to him. He made up his mind to start the next day, but when the next day came, instructions to go immediately to Hamburg arrived from his father. There were rumours of the insolvency of a house with which Mr Palmer dealt; inquiries were necessary which could better be made personally, and if these rumours were correct, as Mr Palmer believed them to be, his agency must be transferred to some other firm. There was now no possibility of a journey to England. For a moment he debated whether, when he was at Hamburg, he could not slip over to London, but it would be dangerous. Further orders might come from his father, and the failure to acknowledge them would lead to evasion, and perhaps to discovery. He must, therefore, content himself with a written explanation to Mrs Caffyn why he could not meet her, and there should be one more effort to make atonement to Madge. This was what went to Mrs Caffyn, and to her lodger: –

Dear Madam, – Your note has reached me here. I am very sorry that my engagements are so pressing that I cannot leave Germany at present. I have written to Miss Hopgood. There is one subject which I cannot mention to her – I cannot speak to her about money. Will you please give me full information? I enclose £20, and I must trust to your discretion. I thank you heartily for all your kindness. – Truly yours,

Frank Palmer

My dearest Madge, – I cannot help saying one more word to you, although, when I last saw you, you told me that it was useless for me to hope. I know, however, that there is now another bond between us, the child is mine as well as yours, and if I am not all that you deserve, ought you to prevent me from doing my duty to it as well as to you? It is true that if we were to marry I could never right you, and perhaps my father would have nothing to do with us, but in time he might relent, and I will come over at once, or, at least, the moment I have settled some business here, and you shall be my wife. Do, my dearest Madge, consent.

When he came to this point his pen stopped. What he had written was very smooth, but very tame and cold. However, nothing better presented itself; he changed his position, sat back in his chair, and searched himself, but could find nothing. It was not always so. Some months ago there would have been no difficulty, and he would not have known when to come to an end. The same thing would have been said a dozen times, perhaps, but it would not have seemed the same to him, and each succeeding repetition would have been felt with the force of novelty. He took a scrap of paper and tried to draft two or three sentences, altered them several times and made them worse. He then re-tread the letter; it was too short; but after all it contained what was necessary, and it must go as it stood. She knew how he felt towards her. So he signed it after giving his address at Hamburg, and it was posted.

Three or four days afterwards Mrs Marshall, in accordance with her usual custom, went to see Madge before she was up. The child lay peacefully by its mother's side and Frank's letter was upon the counterpane. The resolution that no letter from him should be opened had been broken. The two women had become great friends and, within the last few weeks, Madge had compelled Mrs Marshall to call her by her Christian name.

'You've had a letter from Mr Palmer; I was sure it was his handwriting when it came late last night.'

'You can read it; there is nothing private in it.'

She turned round to the child and Mrs Marshall sat down and read. When she had finished she laid the letter on the bed again and was silent.

'Well?' said Madge. 'Would you say "No"?'

'Yes, I would.'

'For your own sake, as well as for his?'

Mrs Marshall took up the letter and read half of it again.

'Yes, you had better say "No." You will find it dull, especially if you have to live in London.'

'Did you find London dull when you came to live in it?'

'Rather; Marshall is away all day long.'

'But scarcely any woman in London expects to marry a man who is not away all day.'

'They ought then to have heaps of work, or they ought to have a lot of children to look after; but, perhaps, being born and bred in the country, I do not know what people in London are. Recollect you were country born and bred yourself, or, at any rate, you have lived in the country for the most of your life.'

'Dull! we must all expect to be dull.'

'There's nothing worse. I've had rheumatic fever, and I say, give me the fever rather than what comes over me at times here. If Marshall had not been so good to me, I do not know what I should have done with myself.'

Madge turned round and looked Mrs Marshall straight in the face, but she did not flinch.

'Marshall is very good to me, but I was glad when mother and you and your sister came to keep me company when he is not at home. It tired me to have my meals alone: it is bad for the digestion; at least, so he says, and he believes that it was indigestion that was the matter with me. I should be sorry for myself if you were to go away; not that I want to put that forward. Maybe I should never see much more of you: he is rich: you might come here sometimes, but he would not like to have Marshall and mother and me at his house.'

Not a word was spoken for at least a minute. Suddenly Mrs Marshall took Madge's hand in her own hands, leaned over her, and in that kind of whisper with which we wake a sleeper who is to be aroused to escape from sudden peril, she said in her ear, –

'Madge, Madge: for God's sake leave him!'

'I have left him.'

'Are you sure?'

'Quite.'

'For ever?'

'For ever!'

Mrs Marshall let go Madge's hand, turned her eyes towards her intently for a moment, and again bent over her as if she were about to embrace her. A knock, however, came at the door, and Mrs Caffyn entered with the cup of coffee which she always insisted on bringing before Madge rose. After she and her daughter had left, Madge read the letter once more. There was nothing new in it, but formally it was something, like the tolling of the bell when we know that our friend is dead. There was a little sobbing, and then she kissed her child with such eagerness that it began to cry.

'You'll answer that letter, I suppose?' said Mrs Caffyn, when they were alone.

'No.'

'I'm rather glad. It would worrit you, and there's nothing worse for a baby than worritin' when it's mother's a-feedin it.'

Mrs Caffyn wrote as follows: –

Dear Sir, – I was sorry as you couldn't come; but I believe now as it was better as you didn't. I am no scollard, and so no more from your obedient, humble servant,

Mrs Caffyn

P.S. – I return the money, having no use for the same.

CHAPTER 22

Baruch did not obtain any very definite information from Marshall about Clara. He was told that she had a sister; that they were both of them gentlewomen; that their mother and father were dead; that they were great readers, and that they did not go to church nor chapel, but that they both went sometimes to hear a certain Mr A. J. Scott* lecture. He was once assistant minister to Irving, but was now heretical, and had a congregation of his own creating at Woolwich.

Baruch called at the shop and found Clara once more alone. The book was packed up and had being lying ready for him for two or three days. He wanted to speak, but hardly knew how to begin. He looked idly round the shelves, taking down one volume after another, and at last he said, –

'I suppose nobody but myself has ever asked for a copy of Robinson?'

'Not since I have been here.'

'I do not wonder at it; he printed only two hundred and fifty; he gave away five-and-twenty, and I am sure nearly two hundred were sold as wastepaper.'

'He is a friend of yours?'

'He was a friend; he is dead; he was an usher in a private school, although you might have supposed, from the title selected, that he was a clerk. I told him it was useless to publish, and his publishers told him the same thing.'

'I should have thought that some notice would have been taken of him; he is so evidently worth it.'

'Yes, but although he was original and reflective, he had no particular talent. His excellence lay in criticism and observation, often profound, on what came to him every day, and he was valueless in the literary market. A talent of some kind is necessary to genius if it is to be heard. So he died utterly unrecognised, save by one or two personal friends who loved him dearly. He was peculiar in the depth and intimacy of his friendships. Few men understand the meaning of the word friendship. They consort with certain companions and perhaps very earnestly admire them, because they possess intellectual gifts, but of friendship, such as we two, Morris and I (for that was his real name) understood it, they know nothing.'*

'Do you believe, that the good does not necessarily survive?'

'Yes and no; I believe that power every moment, so far as our eyes can follow it, is utterly lost. I have had one or two friends whom the world has never known and never will know, who have more in them than is to be found in many an English classic. I could take you to a little dissenting chapel not very far from Holborn where you would hear a young Welshman, with no education beyond that provided by a Welsh denominational college, who is a perfect orator and whose depth of insight is hardly to be matched, save by Thomas À Kempis,* whom he much resembles. When he dies he will be forgotten in a dozen years. Besides, it is surely plain enough to everybody that there are thousands of men and women within a mile of us, apathetic and obscure, who, if, an object worthy of them had been presented to them, would have shown themselves capable of enthusiasm and heroism. Huge volumes of human energy are apparently annihilated.'

'It is very shocking, worse to me than the thought of the earthquake or the pestilence.'

'I said "yes and no" and there is another side. The universe is so wonderful, so intricate, that it is impossible to trace the transformation of its forces, and when they seem to disappear the disappearance may be an illusion. Moreover, "waste" is a word which is applicable only to finite resources. If the resources are infinite it has no meaning.'

Two customers came in and Baruch was obliged to leave. When he came to reflect, he was surprised to find not only how much he had said, but what he had said. He was usually reserved, and with strangers he adhered to the weather or to passing events. He had spoken, however, to this young woman as if they had been acquainted for years. Clara, too, was surprised. She always cut short attempts at conversation in the shop. Frequently she answered questions and receipted and returned bills without looking in the faces of the people who spoke to her or offered her the money. But to this foreigner, or Jew, she had disclosed something she felt. She was rather abashed, but presently her employer, Mr Barnes, returned and somewhat relieved her.

'The gentleman who bought *After Once Hours* came for it while you were out?'

'Oh! what, Cohen? Good fellow Cohen is; he it was who recommended you to me. He is brother-in-law to your landlord.' Clara was comforted; he was not a mere 'casual', as Mr Barnes called his chance customers.

CHAPTER 23

About a fortnight afterwards, on a Sunday afternoon, Cohen went to the Marshalls'. He had called there once or twice since his mother-in-law came to London, but had seen nothing of the lodgers. It was just about tea-time, but unfortunately Marshall and his wife had gone out. Mrs Caffyn insisted that Cohen should stay, but Madge could not be persuaded to come downstairs, and Baruch, Mrs Caffyn and Clara had tea by themselves. Baruch asked Mrs Caffyn if she could endure London after living for so long in the country.

'Ah! my dear boy, I have to like it.'

'No, you haven't; what you mean is that, whether you like it, or whether you do not, you have to put up with it.'

'No, I don't mean that. Miss Hopgood, Cohen and me, we are the best of friends, but whenever he comes here, he allus begins to argue with me. Howsomever, arguing isn't everything, is it, my dear? There's some things, after all, as I can do and he can't, but he's just wrong here in his arguing; that wasn't what I meant. I meant what I said, as I had to like it.'

'How can you like it if you don't?'

'How can I? That shows you're a man and not a woman. Jess like you men. You'd do what you didn't like, I know, for you're a good sort – and everybody would know you didn't like it – but what would be the use of me a-livin' in a house if I didn't like it? – with my daughter and these dear, young women? If it comes to livin', you'd ten thousand times better say at once as you hate bein' where you are than go about all day long, as if you was a blessed saint and put upon.'

Mrs Caffyn twitched at her gown and pulled it down over her knees and brushed the crumbs off with energy. She continued, 'I can't abide people who everlastin' make believe they are put upon. Suppose I were allus a – hankering every foggy day after Great Oakhurst, and yet a-tellin' my daughter as I knew my place was here; if I was she, I should wish my mother at Jericho.'

'Then you really prefer London to Great Oakhurst?' said Clara.

'Why, my dear, of course I do. Don't you think it's pleasanter being here with you and your sister and that precious little creature, and my daughter, than down in that deadalive place? Not that I don't miss my walk sometimes into Darkin; you remember that way as I took you once, Baruch, across the hill, and we went over Ranmore Common and I showed you Camilla Lacy, and you said as you knew a woman who wrote books who once lived there?* You remember them beechwoods? Ah, it was one October! Weren't they a colour – weren't they lovely?'

Baruch remembered them well enough. Who that had ever seen them could forget them?

'And it was I as took you! You wouldn't think it, my dear, though he's always a-arguin', I do believe he'd love to go that walk again, even with an old woman, and see them heavenly beeches. But, Lord, how I do talk, and you've neither of you got any tea.'

'Have you lived long in London, Miss Hopgood?' inquired Baruch.

'Not very long.'

'Do you feel the change?'

'I cannot say I do not.'

'I suppose, however, you have brought yourself to believe in Mrs Caffyn's philosophy?'

'I cannot say that, but I may say that I am scarcely strong enough for mere endurance, and I therefore always endeavour to find something agreeable in circumstances from which there is no escape.'

The recognition of the One in the Many had as great a charm for Baruch as it had for Socrates,* and Clara spoke with the ease of a person whose habit it was to deal with principles and generalisations.

'Yes, and mere toleration, to say nothing of opposition, at least so far as persons are concerned, is seldom necessary. It is generally thought that what is called dramatic power is a poetic gift, but it is really an indispensable virtue to all of us if we are to be happy.'

Mrs Caffyn did not take much interest in abstract statements. 'You remember,' she said, turning to Baruch, 'that man Chorley as has the big farm on the left-hand side just afore you come to the common? He wasn't a Surrey man: he came out of the shires.'

'Very well.'

'He's married that Skelton girl; married her the week afore I left. There isn't no love lost there, but the girl's father said he'd murder him if he didn't, and so it come off. How she ever brought herself to it gets over me. She has that big farm-house, and he's made a fine drawing-room out of the livin' room on the left-hand side as you go in, and put a new grate in the kitchen and turned that into the livin' room, and they does the cooking in the back kitchen, but for all that, if I'd been her, I'd never have seen his face no more, and I'd have packed off to Australia.'

'Does anybody go near them?'

'Near them! of course they do, and, as true as I'm a-sittin' here, our parson, who married them, went to the breakfast. It isn't Chorley as I blame so much; he's a poor, snivellin' creature, and he was frightened, but it's the girl. She doesn't care for him no more than me, and then again, although, as I tell you, he's such a poor creature, he's awful cruel and mean, and she knows it. But what was I a-goin' to say? Never shall I forget that wedding. You know as it's a short cut to the church across the farmyard at the back of my house. The parson, he was rather late – I suppose he'd been giving himself a finishin' touch – and, as it had been very dry weather, he went across the straw and stuff just at the edge like of the yard. There was a pig under the straw – pigs, my dear,' turning to Clara, 'nuzzle under the straw so as you can't see them. Just as he came to this pig it started up and upset him, and he fell and straddled across its back, and the Lord have mercy on me if it didn't carry him at an awful rate, as if he was a jockey at Epsom races, till it come to a puddle of dung water, and then down he plumped in it. You never see'd a man in such a pickle! I heer'd the pig a-squeakin' like mad, and I ran to the door, and I called out to him, and I says, "Mr Ormiston, won't you come in here?" and though, as you know, he allus hated me, he had to come. Mussy on us, how he did stink, and he saw me turn up my nose, and he was wild with rage, and he called the pig a filthy beast. I says to him as that was the pig's way and the pig didn't know who it was who was a-ridin' it, and I took his coat off and wiped his stockings, and sent to the rectory for another coat, and he crept up under the hedge to his garden, and went home, and the people at church had to wait for an hour. I was glad I was goin' away from Great Oakhurst, for he never would have forgiven me.'

There was a ring at the front door bell, and Clara went to see who was there. It was a runaway ring, but she took the opportunity of going upstairs to Madge.

'She has a sister?' said Baruch.

'Yes, and I may just as well tell you about her now – leastways what I know – and I believe as I know pretty near everything about her. You'll have to be told if they stay here. She was engaged to be married, and how it came about with a girl like that is a bit beyond me, anyhow, there's a child, and the father's a good sort by what I can make out, but she won't have anything more to do with him.'

'What do you mean by "a girl like that".'

'She isn't one of them as goes wrong; she can talk German and reads books.'

'Did he desert her?'

'No, that's just it. She loves me, although I say it, as if I was her mother, and yet I'm just as much in the dark as I was the first day I saw her as to why she left that man.'

Mrs Caffyn wiped the corners of her eyes with her apron.

'It's gospel truth as I never took to anybody as I've took to her.'

After Baruch had gone, Clara returned.

'He's a curious creature, my dear,' said Mrs Caffyn, 'as good as gold, but he's too solemn by half. It would do him a world of good if he'd somebody with him who'd make him laugh more. He *can* laugh, for I've seen him forced to get up and hold his sides, but he never makes no noise. He's a Jew, and they say as them as crucified our blessed Lord never laugh proper.'

CHAPTER 24

Baruch was now in love. He had fallen in love with Clara suddenly and totally. His tendency to reflectiveness did not diminish his passion: it rather augmented it. The men and women whose thoughts are here and there continually are not the people to feel the full force of love. Those who do feel it are those who are accustomed to think of one thing at a time, and to think upon it for a long time. 'No man,' said Baruch once 'can love a woman unless he loves God.' 'I should say,' smilingly replied the Gentile, 'that no man can love God unless he loves a woman.' 'I am right,' said Baruch, 'and so are you.'

But Baruch looked in the glass: his hair, jet black when he

was a youth, was marked with grey, and once more the thought
came to him – this time with peculiar force – that he could not
now expect a woman to love him as she had a right to demand
that he should love, and that he must be silent. He was obliged
to call upon Barnes in about a fortnight's time. He still read
Hebrew, and he had seen in the shop a copy of the Hebrew
translation of the *Moreh Nevochim* of Maimonides,* which he
greatly coveted, but could not afford to buy. Like every true
book-lover, he could not make up his mind when he wished for
a book which was beyond his means that he ought once for all
to renounce it, and he was guilty of subterfuges quite unworthy
of such a reasonable creature in order to delude himself into the
belief that he might yield. For example, he wanted a new
overcoat badly, but determined it was more prudent to wait,
and a week afterwards very nearly came to the conclusion that
as he had not ordered the coat he had actually accumulated a
fund from which the *Moreh Nevochim* might be purchased.
When he came to the shop he saw Barnes was there, and he
persuaded himself he should have a quieter moment or two with
the precious volume when Clara was alone. Barnes, of course,
gossiped with everybody.

He therefore called again in the evening, about half an hour
before closing time, and found that Barnes had gone home.
Clara was busy with a catalogue, the proof of which she was
particularly anxious to send to the printer that night. He did
not disturb her, but took down the Maimonides, and for a
few moments was lost in revolving the doctrine, afterwards
repeated and proved by a greater than Maimonides,* that
the will and power of God are co-extensive: that there is
nothing which might be and is not. It was familiar to Baruch,
but like all ideas of that quality and magnitude – and there are
not many of them – it was always new and affected him like a
starry night, seen hundreds of times, yet for ever infinite and
original.

But was it Maimonides which kept him till the porter began
to put up the shutters? Was he pondering exclusively upon God
as the folio lay open before him? He did think about Him, but

whether he would have thought about Him for nearly twenty minutes if Clara had not been there is another matter.

'Do you walk home alone?' he said as she gave the proof to the boy who stood waiting.

'Yes, always.'

'I am going to see Marshall tonight, but I must go to Newman Street first. I shall be glad to walk with you, if you do not mind diverging a little.'

She consented and they went along Oxford Street without speaking, the roar of the carriages and waggons preventing a word.

They turned, however, into Bloomsbury, and were able to hear one another. He had much to say and he could not begin to say it. There was a great mass of something to be communicated pent up within him, and he would have liked to pour it all out before her at once. It is just at such times that we often take up as a means of expression and relief that which is absurdly inexpressive and irrelevant.

'I have not seen your sister yet; I hope I may see her this evening.'

'I hope you may, but she frequently suffers from headache and prefers to be alone.'

'How do you like Mr Barnes?'

The answer is not worth recording, nor is any question or answer which was asked or returned for the next quarter of an hour worth recording, although they were so interesting then. When they were crossing Bedford Square on their return Clara happened to say amongst other commonplaces, –

'What a relief a quiet space in London is.'

'I do not mind the crowd if I am by myself.'

'I do not like crowds; I dislike even the word, and dislike "the masses" still more. I do not want to think of human beings as if they were a cloud of dust, and as if each atom had no separate importance. London is often horrible to me for that reason. In the country it was not quite so bad.'

'That is an illusion,' said Baruch after a moment's pause.

'I do not quite understand you, but if it be an illusion it is very painful. In London human beings seem the commonest, cheapest things in the world, and I am one of them. I went with Mr Marshall not long ago to a Free Trade Meeting,* and more than two thousand people were present. Everybody told me it was magnificent, but it made me very sad.' She was going on, but she stopped. How was it, she thought again, that she could be so communicative? How was it? How is it that sometimes a stranger crosses our path, with whom, before we have known him for more than an hour, we have no secrets? An hour? we have actually known him for centuries.

She could not understand it, and she felt as if she had been inconsistent with her constant professions of wariness in self-revelation.

'It is an illusion, nevertheless – an illusion of the senses. It is difficult to make what I mean clear, because insight is not possible beyond a certain point, and clearness does not come until penetration is complete and what we acquire is brought into a line with other acquisitions. It constantly happens that we are arrested short of this point, but it would be wrong to suppose that our conclusions, if we may call them so, are of no value.'

She was silent, and he did not go on. At last he said, –

'The illusion lies in supposing that number, quantity and terms of that kind are applicable to any other than sensuous objects, but I cannot go further, at least not now. After all, it is possible here in London for one atom to be of eternal import-ance to another.'

They had gone quite round Bedford Square without entering Great Russell Street, which was the way eastwards. A drunken man was holding on by the railings of the Square. He had apparently been hesitating for some time whether he could reach the road, and, just as Baruch and Clara came up to him, he made a lurch towards it, and nearly fell over them. Clara instinctively seized Baruch's arm in order to avoid the poor, staggering mortal; they went once more to the right, and began to complete another circuit. Somehow her arm had been drawn into Baruch's, and there it remained.

'Have you any friends in London?' said Baruch.

'There are Mrs Caffyn, her son and daughter, and there is Mr A. J. Scott. He was a friend of my father.'

'You mean the Mr Scott who was Irving's assistant?'

'Yes.'

'An addition – ' he was about to say, 'an additional bond' but he corrected himself. 'A bond between us; I know Mr Scott.'

'Do you really? I suppose you know many interesting people in London, as you are in his circle.'

'Very few; weeks, months have passed since anybody has said as much to me as you have.'

His voice quivered a little, for he was trembling with an emotion quite inexplicable by mere intellectual relationship. Something came through Clara's glove as her hand rested on his wrist which ran through every nerve and sent the blood into his head.

Clara felt his excitement and dreaded lest he should say something to which she could give no answer, and when they came opposite Great Russell Street, she withdrew her arm from his, and began to cross to the opposite pavement. She turned the conversation towards some indifferent subject, and in a few minutes they were at Great Ormond Street. Baruch would not go in as he had intended; he thought it was about to rain, and he was late. As he went along he became calmer, and when he was fairly indoors he had passed into a despair entirely incon-sistent – superficially – with the philosopher Baruch, as incon-sistent as the irrational behaviour in Bedford Square. He could well enough interpret, so he believed, Miss Hopgood's suppres-sion of him. Ass that he was not to see what he ought to have known so well, that he was playing the fool to her; he, with a grown-up son, to pretend to romance with a girl! At that moment she might be mocking him, or, if she was too good for mockery, she might be contriving to avoid or to quench him. The next time he met her, he would be made to understand that he was *pitied*, and perhaps he would then learn the name of the youth who was his rival, and had won her. He would often meet her, no doubt, but of what value would anything he could say be to her. She could not be expected to make fine distinctions, and there was a class of elderly men, to which of course he would be assigned, but the thought was too horrible. . . .

Perhaps his love for Clara might be genuine; perhaps it was not. He had hoped that as he grew older he might be able really to *see* a woman, but he was once more like one of the possessed. It was not Clara Hopgood who was before him, it was hair, lips, eyes, just as it was twenty years ago, just as it was with the commonest shop-boy he met, who had escaped from the counter, and was waiting at an area gate. It was terrible to him to find that he had so nearly lost his self-control, but upon this point he was unjust to himself, for we are often more distinctly aware of the strength of the temptation than of the authority within us, which falteringly, but decisively, enables us at last to resist it.

Then he fell to meditating how little his studies had done for him. What was the use of them? They had not made him any stronger, and he was no better able than other people to resist temptation. After twenty years' continuous labour he found himself capable of the vulgarest, coarsest faults and failings from which the remotest skiey influence in his begetting might have saved him.

Clara was not as Baruch. No such storm as that which had darkened and disheartened him could pass over her, but she could love, perhaps better than he, and she began to love him. It was very natural to a woman such as Clara, for she had met a man who had said to her that what she believed was really of some worth. Her father and mother had been very dear to her; her sister was very dear to her, but she had never received any such recognition as that which had now been offered to her: her own self had never been returned to her with such honour. She thought, too – why should she not think it? – of the future, of the release from her dreary occupation, of a happy home with independence, and she thought of the children that might be. She lay down without any misgiving. She was sure he was in love with her; she did not know much of him, certainly, in the usual meaning of the word, but she knew enough. She would like to find out more of his history; perhaps without exciting suspicion she might might obtain it from Mrs Caffyn.

CHAPTER 25

Mr Frank Palmer was back again in England. He was much distressed when he received that last letter from Mrs Caffyn, and discovered that Madge's resolution not to write remained unshaken. He was really distressed, but he was not the man upon whom an event, however deeply felt at the time, could score a furrow which could not be obliterated. If he had been a dramatic personage, what had happened to him would have been the second act leading to a fifth, in which the Fates would have appeared, but life seldom arranges itself in proper poetic form. A man determines that he must marry; he makes the shop-girl an allowance, never sees her or her child again, transforms himself into a model husband, is beloved by his wife and family; the woman whom he kissed as he will never kiss his lawful partner, withdraws completely, and nothing happens to him.

Frank was sure he could never love anybody as he had loved Madge, nor could he cut indifferently that other cord which bound him to her. Nobody in society expects the same paternal love for the offspring of a housemaid or a sempstress as for the child of the stockbroker's or brewer's daughter, and nobody expects the same obligations, but Frank was not a society youth, and Madge was his equal. A score of times, when his fancy roved, the rope checked him as suddenly as if it were the lasso of a South American Gaucho. But what could he do? that was the point. There were one or two things which he could have done, perhaps, and one or two things which he could not have done if he had been made of different stuff, but there was nothing more to be done which Frank Palmer could do. After all, it was better that Madge should be the child's mother than that it should belong to some peasant. At least it would be properly educated. As to money, Mrs Caffyn had told him expressly that she did not want it. That might be nothing but pride, and he resolved, without very clearly seeing how, and without troubling himself for the moment as to details, that Madge should be entirely and handsomely supported by him. Meanwhile it was of great importance that he should behave in such a manner as to raise no suspicion. He did not particularly care for some time after his return from Germany to go out to the musical parties to which he was constantly invited, but he went as a duty, and wherever he went he met his charming cousin. They always sang together; they had easy opportunities of practising together, and Frank, although nothing definite was said to him, soon found that his family and hers considered him destined for her. He could not retreat, and there was no surprise manifested by anybody when it was rumoured that they were engaged. His story may as well be finished at once. He and Miss Cecilia Morland were married. A few days before the wedding, when some legal arrangements and settlements were necessary, Frank made one last effort to secure an income for Madge, but it failed. Mrs Caffyn met him by appointment, but he could not persuade her even to be the bearer of a message to Madge. He then determined to confess his fears. To his great relief Mrs Caffyn of her own accord assured him that he never need dread any disturbance or betrayal.

'There are three of us,' she said, 'as knows you – Miss Madge, Miss Clara and myself – and, as far as you are concerned, we are dead and buried. I can't say as I was altogether of Miss Madge's way of looking at it at first, and I thought it ought to have been different, though I believe now as she's right, but,' and the old woman suddenly fired up as if some bolt from heaven had kindled her, 'I pity you, sir – *you*, sir, I say – more nor I do her. You little know what you've lost, the blessedest, sweetest, ah, and the cleverest creature, too, as ever I set eyes on.

'But, Mrs Caffyn,' said Frank, with much emotion, 'it was not I who left her, you know it was not, and, and even – '

The word 'now' was coming, but it did not come.

'Ah,' said Mrs Caffyn, with something like scorn, '*I* know, yes, I do know. It was she, you needn't tell me that, but, God-a-mighty in heaven, if I'd been you, I'd have laid myself on the ground afore her, I'd have tore my heart out for her, and I'd have said, "No other woman in this world but you" – but there, what a fool I am! Goodbye, Mr Palmer.'

She marched away, leaving Frank very miserable, and, as he imagined, unsettled, but he was not so. The fit lasted all day, but when he was walking home that evening, he met a poor friend whose wife was dying.

'I am so grieved,' said Frank 'to hear of your trouble – no hope?'

'None, I am afraid.'

'It is very dreadful.'

Yes, it is hard to bear, but to what is inevitable we must submit.'

This new phrase struck Frank very much, and it seemed very philosophic to him, a maxim for guidance through life. It did not strike him that it was generally either a platitude or an excuse for weakness, and that a nobler duty is to find out what is inevitable and what is not, to declare boldly that what the world oftentimes affirms to be inevitable is really evitable, and heroically to set about making it so. Even if revolt be perfectly useless, we are not particularly drawn to a man who prostrates himself too soon and is incapable of a little cursing.

As it was impossible to provide for Madge and the child now, Frank considered whether he could not do something for them in the will which he had to make before his marriage. He might help his daughter if he could not help the mother.

But his wife would perhaps survive him, and the discovery would cause her and her children much misery; it would damage his character with them and inflict positive moral mischief. The will, therefore, did not mention Madge, and it was not necessary to tell his secret to his solicitor.

The wedding took place amidst much rejoicing; everybody thought the couple were most delightfully matched; the presents were magnificent; the happy pair went to Switzerland, came

back and settled in one of the smaller of the old, red brick
houses in Stoke Newington, with a lawn in front, always shaved
and trimmed to the last degree of smoothness and accuracy,
with paths on whose gravel not the smallest weed was ever seen,
and with a hot-house that provided the most luscious black
grapes. There was a grand piano in the drawing-room, and
Frank and Cecilia became more musical than ever, and Waltham
Lodge was the headquarters of a little amateur orchestra which
practised Mozart and Haydn, and gave local concerts. A twelvemonth after the marriage a son was born and Frank's father
increased Frank's share in the business. Mr Palmer had long
ceased to take any interest in the Hopgoods. He considered that
Madge had treated Frank shamefully in jilting him, but was
convinced that he was fortunate in his escape. It was clear that
she was unstable; she probably threw him overboard for somebody more attractive, and she was not the woman to be a wife
to his son.

One day Cecilia was turning out some drawers belonging to
her husband, and she found a dainty little slipper wrapped up in
white tissue paper. She looked at it for a long time, wondering
to whom it could have belonged, and had half a mind to
announce her discovery to Frank, but she was a wise woman
and forbore. It lay underneath some neckties which were not
now worn, two or three silk pocket handkerchiefs also dis-
carded, and some manuscript books containing school themes.
She placed them on the top of the drawers as if they had all been
taken out in a lump and the slipper was at the bottom.

'Frank my dear,' she said after dinner, 'I emptied this morning
one of the drawers in the attic. I wish you would look over the
things and decide what you wish to keep. I have not examined
them, but they seem to be mostly rubbish.'

He went upstairs after he had smoked his cigar and read his
paper. There was the slipper! It all came back to him, that never-
to-be-forgotten night, when she rebuked him for the folly of
kissing her foot, and he begged the slipper and determined to
preserve it for ever, and thought how delightful it would be to
take it out and look at it when he was an old man. Even now he

did not like to destroy it, but Cecilia might have seen it and might ask him what he had done with it, and what could he say? Finally he decided to burn it. There was no fire, however, in the room, and while he stood meditating, Cecilia called him. He replaced the slipper in the drawer. He could not return that evening, but he intended to go back the next morning, take the little parcel away in his pocket and burn it at his office. At breakfast some letters came which put everything else out of mind. The first thing he did that evening was to revisit the garret, but the slipper had gone. Cecilia had been there and had found it carefully folded up in the drawer. She pulled it out, snipped and tore it into fifty pieces, carried them downstairs, threw them on the dining-room fire, sat down before it, poking them further and further into the flames, and watched them till every vestige had vanished. Frank did not like to make any inquiries; Cecilia made none, and thenceforward no trace existed at Waltham Lodge of Madge Hopgood.

CHAPTER 26

Baruch went neither to Barnes's shop nor to the Marshalls for nearly a month. One Sunday morning he was poring over the *Moreh Nevochim*, for it had proved too powerful a temptation for him, and he fell upon the theorem that without God the Universe could not continue to exist, for God is its Form. It was one of those sayings which may be nothing or much to the reader. Whether it be nothing or much depends upon the quality of his mind.

There was certainly nothing in it particularly adapted to Baruch's condition at that moment, but an antidote may be none the less efficacious because it is not direct. It removed him to another region. It was like the sight and sound of the sea to the man who has been in trouble in an inland city. His self-confidence was restored, for he to whom an idea is revealed becomes the idea, and is no longer personal and consequently poor.

His room seemed too small for him; he shut his book and went to Great Ormond Street. He found there Marshall, Mrs Caffyn, Clara and a friend of Marshall's named Dennis.

'Where is your wife?' said Baruch to Marshall.

'Gone with Miss Madge to the Catholic chapel to hear a mass of Mozart's.'*

'Yes,' said Mrs Caffyn. 'I tell them they'll turn Papists if they do not mind. They are always going to that place, and there's no knowing, so I've hear'd, what them priests can do. They aren't like our parsons. Catch that man at Great Oakhurst a-turnin' anybody.'

'I suppose,' said Baruch to Clara, 'it is the music takes your sister there?'

'Mainly, I believe, but perhaps not entirely.'

'What other attraction can there be?'

'I am not in the least disposed to become a convert. Once for all, Catholicism is incredible and that is sufficient, but there is much in its ritual which suits me. There is no such intrusion of the person of the minister as there is in the Church of England, and still worse amongst dissenters. In the Catholic service the priest is nothing; it is his office which is everything; he is a mere means of communication. The mass, in so far as it proclaims that miracle is not dead, is also very impressive to me.'

'I do not quite understand you,' said Marshall, 'but if you once chuck your reason overboard, you may just as well be Catholic as Protestant. Nothing can be more ridiculous than the Protestant objection, on the ground of absurdity, to the story of the saint walking about with his head under his arm.'

The tea things had been cleared away, and Marshall was smoking. Both he and Dennis were Chartists, and Baruch had interrupted a debate upon a speech delivered at a Chartist meeting that morning by Henry Vincent.*

Frederick Dennis was about thirty, tall and rather loose-limbed. He wore loose clothes, his neck-cloth was tied in a big, loose knot, his feet were large and his boots were heavy. His face was quite smooth, and his hair, which was very thick and light brown, fell across his forehead in a heavy wave with just two complete undulations in it from the parting at the side to the opposite ear. It had a trick of tumbling over his eyes, so that his fingers were continually passed through it to brush it away. He was a wood engraver, or, as he preferred to call himself, an artist, but he also wrote for the newspapers, and had been a contributor to the *Northern Star*.* He was well brought up and was intended for the University, but he did not stick to his Latin and Greek, and as he showed some talent for drawing he was permitted to follow his bent. His work, however, was not of first-rate quality, and consequently orders were not abundant. This was the reason why he had turned to literature. When he had any books to illustrate he lived upon what they brought him, and when there were no books he renewed his acquaintance with politics. If books and newspapers both failed, he subsisted on a little money which had been left him, stayed with friends as long as he could, and amused himself by writing verses which showed much command over rhyme.

'I cannot stand Vincent,' said Marshall, 'he is too flowery for me, and he does not belong to the people. He is middle-class to the backbone.'

'He is deficient in ideas,' said Dennis.

'It is odd,' continued Marshall, turning to Cohen, 'that your race never takes any interest in politics.'

'My race is not a nation, or, if a nation, has no national home. It took an interest in politics when it was in its own country, and produced some rather remarkable political writing.'

'But why do you care so little for what is going on now?'

'I do care, but all people are not born to be agitators, and, furthermore, I have doubts if the Charter will accomplish all you expect.'

'I know what is coming' – Marshall took the pipe out of his mouth and spoke with perceptible sarcasm – 'the inefficiency of merely external remedies, the folly of any attempt at improvement which does not begin with the improvement of individual character, and that those to whom we intend to give power are no better than those from whom we intend to take it away. All very well, Mr Cohen. My answer is that at the present moment the stockingers in Leicester* are earning four shillings and sixpence a week. It is not a question whether they are better or worse than their rulers. They want something to eat, they have nothing, and their masters have more than they can eat.'

'Apart altogether from purely material reasons,' said Dennis, 'we have rights; we are born into this planet without our consent, and, therefore, we may make certain demands.'

'Do you not think,' said Clara, 'that the repeal of the corn laws will help you?'

Dennis smiled and was about to reply, but Marshall broke out savagely, –

'Repeal of the corn laws is a contemptible device of manufacturing selfishness. It means low wages. Do you suppose the great Manchester cotton lords care one straw for their hands? Not they! They will face a revolution for repeal because it will enable them to grind an extra profit out of us.'

'I agree with you entirely,' said Dennis, turning to Clara, 'that a tax upon food is wrong; it is wrong in the abstract. The notion of taxing bread, the fruit of the earth, is most repulsive; but the point is – what is our policy to be? If a certain end is to be achieved, we must neglect subordinate ends, and, at times, even contradict what our own principles would appear to dictate. That is the secret of successful leadership.'

He took up the poker and stirred the fire.

'That will do, Dennis,' said Marshall, who was evidently fidgety. 'The room is rather warm. There's nothing in Vincent which irritates me more than those bits of poetry with which he winds up.

God made the man – man made the slave,*

and all that stuff. If God made the man, God made the slave. I know what Vincent's little game is, and it is the same game with all his set. They want to keep Chartism religious, but we shall see. Let us once get the six points, and the Established Church will go, and we shall have secular education, and in a generation there will not be one superstition left.'

'Theological superstition, you mean?' said Clara.

'Yes, of course, what others are there worth notice?'

'A few. The superstition of the ordinary newspaper reader is just as profound, and the tyranny of the majority may be just as injurious as the superstition of a Spanish peasant, or the tyranny of the Inquisition.'

'Newspapers will not burn people as the priests did and would do again if they had the power, and they do not insult us with fables and a hell and a heaven.'

'I maintain,' said Clara with emphasis, 'that if a man declines to examine, and takes for granted what a party leader or a newspaper tells him, he has no case against the man who declines to examine, or takes for granted what the priest tells him. Besides, although, as you know, I am not a convert myself, I do lose a little patience when I hear it preached as a gospel to every poor conceited creature who goes to your Sunday evening atheist lecture, that he is to believe nothing on one particular subject which his own precious intellect cannot verify, and the next morning he finds it to be his duty to swallow wholesale anything you please to put into his mouth. As to the tyranny, the day may come, and I believe is approaching, when the majority will be found to be more dangerous than any ecclesiastical establishment which ever existed.'

Baruch's lips moved, but he was silent. He was not strong in argument. He was thinking about Marshall's triumphant inquiry whether God is not responsible for slavery. He would have liked to say something on that subject, but he had nothing ready.

'Practical people,' said Dennis, who had not quite recovered from the rebuke as to the warmth of the room, 'are often most unpractical and injudicious. Nothing can be more unwise than to mix up politics and religion. If you *do*,' Dennis waved his hand, 'you will have all the religious people against you. My friend Marshall, Miss Hopgood, is under the illusion that the Church in this country is tottering to its fall. Now, although I myself belong to no sect, I do not share his illusion; nay, more, I am not sure' – Mr Dennis spoke slowly, rubbed his chin and looked up at the ceiling – 'I am not sure that there is not something to be said in favour of State endowment – at least, in a country like Ireland.'

'Come along, Dennis, we shall be late,' said Marshall, and the two forthwith took their departure in order to attend another meeting.

'Much either of 'em knows about it,' said Mrs Caffyn when they had gone. 'There's Marshall getting two pounds a week reg'lar, and goes on talking about people at Leicester, and he has never been in Leicester in his life; and, as for that Dennis, he knows less than Marshall, for he does nothing but write for newspapers and draw for picture-books, never nothing what you may call work, and he does worrit me so whenever he begins about poor people that I can't sit still. *I* do know what the poor is, having lived at Great Oakhurst all these years.'

'You are not a Chartist, then?' said Baruch.

'Me – me a Chartist? No, I ain't, and yet, maybe, I'm something worse. What would be the use of giving them poor creatures votes? Why, there isn't one of them as wouldn't hold up his hand for anybody as would give him a shilling. Quite right of 'em, too, for the one thing they have to think about from morning to night is how to get a bit of something to fill their bellies, and they won't fill them by voting.'

'But what would you do for them?'

'Ah! that beats me! Hang somebody, but I don't know who it ought to be. There's a family by the name of Longwood, they live just on the slope of the hill nigh the Dower Farm, and there's nine of them, and the youngest when I left was a baby six months old, and their living-room faces the road so that the north wind blows in right under the door, and I've seen the snow lie in heaps inside. As reg'lar as winter comes Longwood is knocked off – no work. I've knowed them not have a bit of meat for weeks together, and him a-loungin' about at the corner of the street. Wasn't that enough to make him feel as if somebody ought to be killed? And Marshall and Dennis say as the proper thing to do is to give him a vote, and prove to him there was never no Abraham nor Isaac, and that Jonah never was in a whale's belly, and that nobody had no business to have more children than he could feed. And what goes on, and what must go on, inside such a place as Longwood's, with him and his wife, and with them boys and gals all huddled together – But I'd better hold my tongue. We'll let the smoke out of this room, I think, and air it a little.'

She opened the window, and Baruch rose and went home.

Whenever Mrs Caffyn talked about the labourers at Great Oakhurst, whom she knew so well, Clara always felt as if all her reading had been a farce, and, indeed, if we come into close contact with actual life, art, poetry and philosophy seem little better than trifling.* When the mist hangs over the heavy clay land in January, and men and women shiver in the bitter cold and eat raw turnips, to indulge in fireside ecstasies over the divine Plato or Shakespeare is surely not such a virtue as we imagine it to be.

CHAPTER 27

Baruch sat and mused before he went to bed. He had gone out stirred by an idea, but it was already dead. Then he began to think about Clara. Who was this Dennis who visited the Marshalls and the Hopgoods? Oh! for an hour of his youth! Fifteen years ago the word would have come unbidden if he had seen Clara, but now, in place of the word, there was hesitation, shame. He must make up his mind to renounce for ever. But, although this conclusion had forced itself upon him overnight as inevitable, he could not resist the temptation when he rose the next morning of plotting to meet Clara, and he walked up and down the street opposite the shop door that evening nearly a quarter of an hour, just before closing time, hoping that she might come out and that he might have the opportunity of overtaking her apparently by accident. At last, fearing he might

miss her, he went in and found she had a companion whom he
instantly knew, before any introduction, to be her sister. Madge
was not now the Madge whom we knew at Fenmarket. She was
thinner in the face and paler. Nevertheless, she was not careless;
she was even more particular in her costume, but it was simpler.
If anything, perhaps, she was a little prouder. She was more
attractive, certainly, than she had ever been, although her face
could not be said to be handsomer. The slight prominence of
the cheek-bone, the slight hollow underneath, the loss of colour,
were perhaps defects, but they said something which had a
meaning in it superior to that of the tint of the peach. She had
been reading a book while Clara was balancing her cash, and
she attempted to replace it. The shelf was a little too high, and
the volume fell upon the ground. It contained Shelley's *Revolt
of Islam*.*

'Have you read Shelley?' said Baruch.

'Every line – when I was much younger.'

'Do you read him now?'

'Not much. I was an enthusiast for him when I was nineteen,
but I find that his subject matter is rather thin, and his themes
are a little worn. He was entirely enslaved by the ideals of the
French Revolution. Take away what the French Revolution
contributed to his poetry, and there is not much left.'

'As a man he is not very attractive to me.'

'Nor to me; I never shall forgive his treatment of Harriet.'

'I suppose he had ceased to love her, and he thought,
therefore, he was justified in leaving her.'

Madge turned and fixed her eyes, unobserved, on Baruch. He
was looking straight at the bookshelves. There was not, and,
indeed, how could there be, any reference to herself.

'I should put it in this way,' she said, 'that he thought he was
justified in sacrificing a woman for the sake of an *impulse*. Call
this a defect or a crime – whichever you like – it is repellent to
me. It makes no difference to me to know that he believed the
impulse to be divine.'

'I wish,' interrupted Clara, 'you two would choose less
exciting subjects of conversation; my totals will not come right.'

They were silent, and Baruch, affecting to study a Rollin's *Ancient History*,* wondered, especially when he called to mind Mrs Caffyn's report, what this girl's history could have been. He presently recovered himself, and it occurred to him that he ought to give some reason why he had called. Before, however, he was able to offer any excuse, Clara closed her book.

'Now, it is right,' she said, 'and I am ready.'

Just at that moment Barnes appeared, hot with hurrying.

'Very sorry, Miss Hopgood, to ask you to stay for a few minutes. I recollected after I left that the doctor particularly wanted those books sent off tonight. I should not like to disappoint him. I have been to the booking-office, and the van will be here in about twenty minutes. If you will make out the invoice and check me, I will pack them.'

'I will be off,' said Madge. 'The shop will be shut if I do not make haste.'

'You are not going alone, are you?' said Baruch. 'May I not go with you, and cannot we both come back for your sister?'

'It is very kind of you.'

Clara looked up from her desk, watched them as they went out at the door and, for a moment, seemed lost. Barnes turned round.

'Now, Miss Hopgood.' She started.

'Yes, sir.'

'*Fabricius, J. A. Bibliotheca Ecclesiastica in qua continentur.*'*

'I need not put in the last three words.'

'Yes, yes.' Barnes never liked to be corrected in a title. 'There's another *Fabricius Bibliotheca* or *Bibliographia*. Go on – *Basili opera ad MSS. codices,* 3 vols.'

Clara silently made the entries a little more scholarly. In a quarter of an hour the parcel was ready and Cohen returned.

'Your sister would not allow me to wait. She met Mrs Marshall; they said they should have something to carry, and that it was not worth while to bring it here. I will walk with you, if you will allow me. We may as well avoid Holborn.'

They turned into Gray's Inn, and, when they were in comparative quietude, he said, –

'Any Chartist news?' and then without waiting for an answer, 'By the way, who is your friend Dennis?'

'He is no particular friend of mine. He is a wood-engraver, and writes also, I believe, for the newspapers.'

'He can talk as well as write.'

'Yes, he can talk very well.'

'Do you not think there was something unreal about what he said?'

'I do not believe he is actually insincere. I have noticed that men who write or read much often appear somewhat shadowy.'

'How do you account for it?'

'What they say is not experience.'

'I do not quite understand. A man may think much which can never become an experience in your sense of the word, and be very much in earnest with what he thinks; the thinking is an experience.'

'Yes, I suppose so, but it is what a person has gone through which I like to hear. Poor Dennis has suffered much. You are perhaps surprised, but it is true, and when he leaves politics alone he is a different creature.'

'I am afraid I must be very uninteresting to you?'

'I did not mean that I care for nothing but my friend's aches and pains, but that I do not care for what he just takes up and takes on.'

'It is my misfortune that my subjects are not very – I was about to say – human. Perhaps it is because I am a Jew.'

'I do not know quite what you mean by your "subjects", but if you mean philosophy and religion, they are human.'

'If they are, very few people like to hear anything about them. Do you know, Miss Hopgood, I can never talk to anybody as I can to you.'

Clara made no reply. A husband was to be had for a look, for a touch, a husband whom she could love, a husband who could give her all her intellect demanded. A little house rose before her eyes as if by Arabian enchantment; there was a bright fire on the hearth, and there were children round it; without the look, the touch, there would be solitude, silence and a childless old age, so much more to be feared by a woman than by a man. Baruch paused, waiting for her answer, and her tongue actually began to move with a reply, which would have sent his arm round her, and made them one for ever, but it did not come. Something fell and flashed before her like lightning from a cloud overhead, divinely beautiful, but divinely terrible.

'I remember,' she said, 'that I have to call in Lamb's Conduit Street to buy something for my sister. I shall just be in time.' Baruch went as far as Lamb's Conduit Street with her. He, too, would have determined his own destiny if she had uttered the word, but the power to proceed without it was wanting and he fell back. He left her at the door of the shop. She bid him goodbye, obviously intending that he should go no further with her, and he shook hands with her, taking her hand again and shaking it again with a grasp which she knew well enough was too fervent for mere friendship. He then wandered back once more to his old room at Clerkenwell. The fire was dead, he stirred it, the cinders fell through the grate and it dropped out all together. He made no attempt to rekindle it, but sat staring at the black ashes, not thinking, but dreaming. Thirty years more perhaps with no change! The last chance that he could begin a new life had disappeared. He cursed himself that nothing drove him out of himself with Marshall and his fellow-men; that he was not Chartist nor revolutionary; but it was impossible to create in himself enthusiasm for a cause. He had tried before to become a patriot and had failed, and was conscious, during the trial, that he was pretending to be something he was not and could not be. There was nothing to be done but to pace the straight road in front of him, which led nowhere, so far as he could see.

CHAPTER 28

A month afterwards Marshall announced that he intended to pay a visit.

'I am going,' he said, 'to see Mazzini.* Who will go with me?'

Clara and Madge were both eager to accompany him. Mrs Caffyn and Mrs Marshall chose to stay at home.

'I shall ask Cohen to come with us,' said Marshall. 'He has never seen Mazzini and would like to know him. Cohen accordingly called one Sunday evening, and the party went together to a dull, dark, little house in a shabby street of small shops and furnished apartments. When they knocked at Mazzini's door Marshall asked for Mr—for, even in England, Mazzini had an assumed name which was always used when inquiries were made for him. They were shown upstairs into a rather mean room, and found there a man, really about forty, but looking older. He had dark hair growing away from his forehead, dark moustache, dark beard and a singularly serious face. It was not the face of a conspirator, but that of a saint, although without that just perceptible touch of silliness which spoils the faces of most saints. It was the face of a saint of the Reason, of a man who could be ecstatic for rational ideals, rarest of all endowments. It was the face, too, of one who knew no fear, or, if he knew it, could crush it. He was once concealed by a poor woman whose house was surrounded by Austrian soldiers watching for him. He was determined that she should not be sacrificed, and, having disguised himself a little, walked out into the street in broad daylight, went up to the Austrian sentry, asked for a light for his cigar and escaped. He was cordial in his reception of his visitors, particularly of Clara, Madge and Cohen, whom he had not seen before.

'The English,' he said, after some preliminary conversation, 'are a curious people. As a nation they are what they call practical and have a contempt for ideas, but I have known some Englishmen who have a religious belief in them, a nobler belief than I have found in any other nation. There are English women, also, who have this faith, and one or two are amongst my dearest friends.'

'I never,' said Marshall, 'quite comprehend you on this point. I should say that we know as clearly as most folk what we want, and we mean to have it.'

'That may be, but it is not Justice, as Justice which inspires you. Those of you who have not enough, desire to have more, that is all.'

'If we are to succeed, we must preach what the people understand.'

'Pardon me, that is just where you and I differ. Whenever any real good is done it is by a crusade; that is to say, the cross must be raised and appeal be made to something *above* the people. No system based on rights will stand. Never will society be permanent till it is founded on duty. If we consider our rights exclusively, we extend them over the rights of our neighbours. If the oppressed classes had the power to obtain their rights tomorrow, and with the rights came no deeper sense of duty, the new order, for the simple reason that the oppressed are no better than their oppressors, would be just as unstable as that which preceded it.'

'To put it in my own language,' said Madge, 'you believe in God.'

Mazzini leaned forward and looked earnestly at her.

'My dear young friend, without that belief I should have no other.'

'I should like, though,' said Marshall, 'to see the church which would acknowledge you and Miss Madge, or would admit your God to be theirs.'

'What is essential,' replied Madge, 'in a belief in God is absolute loyalty to a principle we know to have authority.'

'It may, perhaps,' said Mazzini, 'be more to me, but you are right, it is a belief in the supremacy and ultimate victory of the conscience.'

'The victory seems distant in Italy now,' said Baruch. 'I do not mean the millennial victory of which you speak, but an approximation to it by the overthrow of tyranny there.'

'You are mistaken; it is far nearer than you imagine.'

'Do you obtain,' said Clara, 'any real help from people here? Do you not find that they merely talk and express what they call their sympathy?'

'I must not say what help I have received; more than words, though, from many.'

'You expect, then,' said Baruch, 'that the Italians will answer your appeal?'

'If I had no faith in the people, I do not see what faith could survive.'

'The people are the persons you meet in the street.'

'A people is not a mere assemblage of uninteresting units, but it is not a phantom. A spirit lives in each nation which is superior to any individual in it. It is this which is the true reality, the nation's purpose and destiny, it is this for which the patriot lives and dies.'

'I suppose,' said Clara, 'you have no difficulty in obtaining volunteers for any dangerous enterprise?'

'None. You would be amazed if I were to tell you how many men and women at this very moment would go to meet certain death if I were to ask them.'

'Women?'

'Oh, yes; and women are of the greatest use, but it is rather difficult to find those who have the necessary qualifications.'

'I suppose you employ them in order to obtain secret information?'

'Yes; amongst the Austrians.'

The party broke up. Baruch manœuvred to walk with Clara, but Marshall wanted to borrow a book from Mazzini, and she stayed behind for him. Madge was outside in the street, and Baruch could do nothing but go to her. She seemed unwilling to wait, and Baruch and she went slowly homewards, thinking the others would overtake them. The conversation naturally turned upon Mazzini.

'Although,' said Madge, 'I have never seen him before, I have heard much about him and he makes me sad.'

'Why?'

'Because he has done something worth doing and will do more.'

'But why should that make you sad?'

'I do not think there is anything sadder than to know you are able to do a little good and would like to do it, and yet you are not permitted to do it. Mazzini has a world open to him large enough for the exercise of all his powers.'

'It is worse to have a desire which is intense but not definite, to be continually anxious to do something, you know not what, and always to feel, if any distinct task is offered, your incapability of attempting it.'

'A man, if he has a real desire to be of any service, can generally gratify it to some extent; a woman as a rule cannot, although a woman's enthusiasm is deeper than a man's. You can join Mazzini tomorrow, I suppose, if you like.'

'It is a supposition not quite justifiable, and if I were free to go I could not.'

'Why?'

'I am not fitted for such work; I have not sufficient faith. When I see a flag waving, a doubt always intrudes. Long ago I was forced to the conclusion that I should have to be content with a life which did not extend outside itself.'

'I am sure that many women blunder into the wrong path, not because they are bad, but simply because – if I may say so – they are too good.'

'Maybe you are right. The inability to obtain mere pleasure has not produced the misery which has been begotten of mistaken or baffled self-sacrifice. But do you mean to say that you would like to enlist under Mazzini?'

'No!'

Baruch thought she referred to her child, and he was silent.

'You are a philosopher,' said Madge, after a pause. 'Have you never discovered anything which will enable us to submit to be useless?'

'That is to say, have I discovered a religion? for the core of religion is the relationship of the individual to the whole, the faith that the poorest and meanest of us is a person. That is the real strength of all religions.'

'Well, go on; what do you believe?'

'I can only say it like a creed; I have no demonstration, at least none such as I would venture to put into words. Perhaps the highest of all truths is incapable of demonstration and can only be stated. Perhaps, also, the statement, at least to some of us, is a sufficient demonstration. I believe that inability to imagine a thing is not a reason for its non-existence. If the infinite is a conclusion which is forced upon me, the fact that I cannot picture it does not disprove it. I believe, also, in thought and the soul, and it is nothing to me that I cannot explain them by attributes belonging to body. That being so, the difficulties which arise from the perpetual and unconscious confusion of the qualities of thought and soul with those of body disappear. Our imagination represents to itself souls like pebbles, and asks itself what count can be kept of a million, but number in such a case is inapplicable. I believe that all thought is a manifestation of the Being, who is One, whom you may call God if you like, and that, as It never was created, It will never be destroyed.'

'But,' said Madge, interrupting him, 'although you began by warning me not to expect that you would prove anything, you can tell me whether you have any kind of basis for what you say, or whether it is all a dream.'

'You will be surprised, perhaps, to hear that mathematics, which, of course, I had to learn for my own business, have supplied something for a foundation. They lead to ideas which are inconsistent with the notion that the imagination is a measure of all things. Mind, I do not for a moment pretend that I have any theory which explains the universe. It is something, however, to know that the sky is as real as the earth.'

They had now reached Great Ormond Street, and parted. Clara and Marshall were about five minutes behind them. Madge was unusually cheerful when they sat down to supper.

'Clara,' she said, 'what made you so silent tonight at

Mazzini's?' Clara did not reply, but after a pause of a minute or two, she asked Mrs Caffyn whether it would not be possible for them all to go into the country on Whitmonday? Whitsuntide was late; it would be warm, and they could take their food with them and eat it out of doors.

'Just the very thing, my dear, if we could get anything cheap to take us; the baby, of course, must go with us.

'I should like above everything to go to Great Oakhurst.'

'What, five of us – twenty miles there and twenty miles back! Besides, although I love the place, it isn't exactly what one would go to see just for a day. No! Letherhead or Mickleham or Darkin would be ever so much better. They are too far, though, and, then, that man Baruch must go with us. He'd be company for Marshall, and he sticks up in Clerkenwell and never goes nowhere. You remember as Marshall said as he must ask him the next time we had an outing.'

Clara had not forgotten it.

'Ah,' continued Mrs Caffyn, 'I should just love to show you Mickleham.'

Mrs Caffyn's heart yearned after her Surrey land. The man who is born in a town does not know what it is to be haunted through life by lovely visions of the landscape which lay about him when he was young. The village youth leaves the home of his childhood for the city, but the river doubling on itself, the overhanging alders and willows, the fringe of level meadow, the chalk hills bounding the river valley and rising against the sky, with here and there on their summits solitary clusters of beech, the light and peace of the different seasons, of morning, afternoon and evening, never forsake him. To think of them is not a mere luxury; their presence modifies the whole of his life.

'I don't see how it is to be managed,' she mused; 'and yet there's nothing near London as I'd give two pins to see. There's Richmond as we went to one Sunday; it was no better, to my way of thinking, than looking at a picture. I'd ever so much sooner be a-walking across the turnips by the footpath from Darkin home.'

'Couldn't we, for once in a way, stay somewhere over-night?'

'It might as well be two,' said Mrs Marshall; 'Saturday and Sunday.'

'Two,' said Madge; 'I vote for two.'

'Wait a bit, my dears, we're a precious awkward lot to fit in – Marshall and his wife; me and you and Miss Clara and the baby; and then there's Baruch, who's odd man, so to speak; that's three bedrooms. We sha'n't do it – Otherwise, I was a-thinking – '

'What were you thinking?' said Marshall.

'I've got it,' said Mrs Caffyn, joyously. ' Miss Clara and me will go to Great Oakhurst on the Friday. We can easy enough stay at my old shop. Marshall and Sarah, Miss Madge, the baby and Baruch can go to Letherhead on the Saturday morning. The two women and the baby can have one of the rooms at Skelton's, and Marshall and Baruch can have the other. Then, on Sunday morning, Miss Clara and me we'll come over for you, and we'll all walk through Norbury Park. That'll be ever so much better in many ways. Miss Clara and me, we'll go by the coach. Six of us, not reckoning the baby, in that heavy ginger-beer cart of Masterman's would be too much.'

'An expensive holiday, rather,' said Marshall.

'Leave that to me; that's my business. I ain't quite a beggar, and if we can't take our pleasure once a year, it's a pity. We aren't like some folk as messes about up to Hampstead every Sunday, and spends a fortune on shrimps and donkeys. No; when I go away, it *is* away, maybe it's only for a couple of days, where I can see a blessed ploughed field; no shrimps nor donkeys for me.'

CHAPTER 29

So it was settled, and on the Friday Clara and Mrs Caffyn journeyed to Great Oakhurst. They were both tired, and went to bed very early, in order that they might enjoy the next day.

Clara, always a light sleeper, woke between three and four, rose and went to the little casement window which had been open all night. Below her, on the left, the church was just discernible, and on the right, the broad chalk uplands leaned to the south, and were waving with green barley and wheat. Underneath her lay the cottage garden, with its row of beehives in the north-east corner, sheltered from the cold winds by the thick hedge. It had evidently been raining a little, for the drops hung on the currant bushes, but the clouds had been driven by the south-westerly wind into the eastern sky, where they lay in a long, low, grey band. Not a sound was to be heard, save every now and then the crow of a cock or the short cry of a just-awakened thrush. High up on the zenith, the approach of the sun to the horizon was proclaimed by the most delicate tints of rose-colour, but the cloud-bank above him was dark and untouched, although the blue which was over it, was every moment becoming paler. Clara watched; she was moved even to tears by the beauty of the scene, but she was stirred by something more than beauty, just as he who was in the Spirit and beheld a throne and One sitting thereon, saw something more than loveliness, although He was radiant with the colour of jasper and there was a rainbow round about Him like an emerald to look upon.* In a few moments the highest top of the cloud-rampart was kindled, and the whole wavy outline became a fringe of flame. In a few moments more the fire just at one point became blinding, and in another second the sun emerged, the first arrowy shaft passed into her chamber, the first shadow was cast, and it was day. She put her hands to her face; the tears fell faster, but she wiped them away and her great purpose was fixed. She crept back into bed, her agitation ceased, a strange and almost supernatural peace overshadowed her and she fell asleep not to wake till the sound of the scythe had ceased in the meadow just beyond the rick-yard that came up to one side of the cottage, and the mowers were at their breakfast.

Neither Mrs Caffyn nor Clara thought of seeing the Letherhead party on Saturday. They could not arrive before the afternoon, and it was considered hardly worth while to walk

from Great Oakhurst to Letherhead merely for the sake of an
hour or two. In the morning Mrs Caffyn was so busy with her
old friends that she rather tired herself, and in the evening Clara
went for a stroll. She did not know the country, but she
wandered on until she came to a lane which led down to the
river. At the bottom of the lane she found herself at a narrow,
steep, stone bridge. She had not been there more than three or
four minutes before she descried two persons coming down the
lane from Letherhead. When they were about a couple of
hundred yards from her they turned into the meadow over the
stile, and struck the river-bank some distance below the point
where she was. It was impossible to mistake them; they were
Madge and Baruch. They sauntered leisurely; presently Baruch
knelt down over the water, apparently to gather something
which he gave to Madge. They then crossed another stile and
were lost behind the tall hedge which stopped further view of
the footpath in that direction.

'The message then was authentic,' she said to herself. 'I
thought I could not have misunderstood it.'

On Sunday morning Clara wished to stay at home. She
pleaded that she preferred rest, but Mrs Caffyn vowed there
should be no Norbury Park if Clara did not go, and the kind
creature managed to persuade a pig-dealer to drive them over to
Letherhead for a small sum, notwithstanding it was Sunday.
The whole party then set out; the baby was drawn in a borrowed
carriage which also took the provisions, and they were fairly out
of the town before the Letherhead bells had ceased ringing for
church. It was one of the sweetest of Sundays, sunny, but masses
of white clouds now and then broke the heat. The park was
reached early in the forenoon, and it was agreed that dinner
should be served under one of the huge beech trees at the lower
end, as the hill was a little too steep for the baby-carriage in the
hot sun.

'This is very beautiful,' said Marshall, when dinner was over,
'but it is not what we came to see. We ought to move upwards
to the Druid's grove.'

'Yes, you be off, the whole lot of you,' said Mrs Caffyn. 'I know every tree there, and I ain't going there this afternoon. Somebody must stay here to look after the baby; you can't wheel her, you'll have to carry her, and you won't enjoy yourselves much more for moiling along with her up that hill.'

'I will stay with you,' said Clara.

Everybody protested, but Clara was firm. She was tired, and the sun had given her a headache. Madge pleaded that it was she who ought to remain behind, but at last gave way for her sister looked really fatigued.

'There's a dear child,' said Clara, when Madge consented to go. 'I shall lie on the grass and perhaps go to sleep.'

'It is a pity,' said Baruch to Madge as they went away, 'that we are separated; we must come again.'

'Yes, I am sorry, but perhaps it is better she should be where she is; she is not particularly strong, and is obliged to be very careful.'

In due time they all came to the famous yews, and sat down on one of the seats overlooking that wonderful gate in the chalk downs through which the Mole passes northwards.

'We must go,' said Marshall, 'a little bit further and see the oak.'

'Not another step,' said his wife. 'You can go if you like.'

'Content; nothing could be pleasanter than to sit here,' and he pulled out his pipe; 'but really, Miss Madge, to leave Norbury without paying a visit to the oak is a pity.'

He did not offer, however, to accompany her.

'It is the most extraordinary tree in these parts,' said Baruch; 'of incalculable age and with branches spreading into a tent big enough to cover a regiment. Marshall is quite right.'

'Where is it?'

'Not above a couple of hundred yards further; just round the corner.'

Madge rose and looked.

'No; it is not visible here; it stands a little way back. If you come a little further you will catch a glimpse of it.'

She followed him and presently the oak came in view. They climbed up the bank and went nearer to it. The whole vale was underneath them and part of the weald with the Sussex downs blue in the distance. Baruch was not much given to raptures over scenery, but the indifference of Nature to the world's turmoil always appealed to him.

'You are not now discontented because you cannot serve under Mazzini?'

'Not now.'

There was nothing in her reply on the face of it of any particular consequence to Baruch. She might simply have intended that the beauty of the fair landscape extinguished her restlessness, or that she saw her own unfitness, but neither of these interpretations presented itself to him.

'I have sometimes thought,' continued Baruch, slowly, 'that the love of any two persons in this world may fulfil an eternal purpose which is as necessary to the Universe as a great revolution.'

Madge's eyes moved round from the hills and they met Baruch's. No syllable was uttered, but swiftest messages passed, question and answer. There was no hesitation on his part now, no doubt, the woman and the moment had come. The last question was put, the final answer was given; he took her hand in his and came closer to her.

'Stop!' she whispered, 'do you know my history?'

He did not reply, but fell upon her neck. This was the goal to which both had been journeying all these years, although with much weary mistaking of roads; this was what from the beginning was designed for both! Happy Madge! happy Baruch! There are some so closely akin that the meaning of each may be said to lie in the other, who do not approach till it is too late. They travel towards one another, but are waylaid and detained, and just as they are within greeting, one of them drops and dies.

They left the tree and went back to the Marshalls, and then down the hill to Mrs Caffyn and Clara. Clara was much better for her rest, and early in the evening the whole party returned to Letherhead, Clara and Mrs Caffyn going on to Great Oakhurst.

Madge kept close to her sister till they separated, and the two men walked together. On Whitmonday morning the Letherhead people came over to Great Oakhurst. They had to go back to London in the afternoon, but Mrs Caffyn and Clara were to stay till Tuesday, as they stood a better chance of securing places by the coach on that day. Mrs Caffyn had as much to show them as if the village had been the Tower of London. The wonder of wonders, however, was a big house, where she was well known, and its hot-houses. Madge wanted to speak to Clara, but it was difficult to find a private opportunity. When they were in the garden, however, she managed to take Clara unobserved down one of the twisted paths, under pretence of admiring an ancient mulberry tree.

'Clara,' she said, 'I want a word with you. Baruch Cohen loves me.'

'Do you love him?'

'Yes.'

'Without a shadow of a doubt?'

'Without a shadow of a doubt.'

Clara put her arm round her sister, kissed her tenderly and said, – '

'Then I am perfectly happy.'

'Did you suspect it?'

'I knew it.'

Mrs Caffyn called them; it was time to be moving, and soon afterwards those who had to go to London that afternoon left for Letherhead. Clara stood at the gate for a long time watching them along the straight, white road. They came to the top of the hill; she could just discern them against the sky; they passed over the ridge and she went indoors. In the evening a friend called to see Mrs Caffyn, and Clara went to the stone bridge which she had visited on Saturday. The water on the upper side of the bridge was dammed up and fell over the little sluice gates under the arches into a clear and deep basin about forty or fifty feet in diameter. The river, for some reason of its own, had bitten into the western bank, and had scooped out a great piece of it into an island. The main current went round the island with a shallow, swift ripple, instead of going through the pool,

as it might have done, for there was a clear channel for it. The
centre and the region under the island were deep and still, but
at the farther end, where the river in passing called to the pool,
it broke into waves as it answered the appeal, and added its own
contribution to the stream, which went away down to the mill
and onwards to the big Thames. On the island were aspens and
alders. The floods had loosened the roots of the largest tree, and
it hung over heavily in the direction in which it had yielded to
the rush of the torrent, but it still held its grip, and the sap had
not forsaken a single branch. Every one was as dense with
foliage as if there had been no struggle for life, and the leaves
sang their sweet song, just perceptible for a moment every now
and then in the variations of the louder music below them. It is
curious that the sound of a weir is never uniform, but is
perpetually changing in the ear even of a person who stands
close by it. One of the arches of the bridge was dry, and Clara
went down into it, stood at the edge and watched that wonderful
sight – the plunge of a smooth, pure stream into the great cup
which it has hollowed out for itself. Down it went, with a
dancing, foamy fringe playing round it just where it met the
surface; a dozen yards away it rose again, bubbling and exultant.

She came up from the arch and went home as the sun was
setting. She found Mrs Caffyn alone.

'I have news to tell you,' she said. 'Baruch Cohen is in love
with my sister, and she is in love with him.'

'The Lord, Miss Clara! I thought sometimes that perhaps it
might be you; but there, it's better, maybe, as it is, for – '

'For what?'

'Why, my dear, because somebody's sure to turn up who'll
make you happy, but there aren't many men like Baruch. You
see what I mean, don't you? He's always a-reading books, and,
therefore, he don't think so much of what some people would
make a fuss about. Not as anything of that kind would ever stop
me, if I were a man and saw such a woman as Miss Madge.
He's really as good a creature as ever was born, and with that
child she might have found it hard to get along, and now it will
be cared for, and so will she be to the end of their lives.'

The evening after their return to Great Ormond Street, Mazzini was surprised by a visit from Clara alone.

'When I last saw you,' she said, 'you told us that you had been helped by women. I offer myself.'

'But, my dear madam, you hardly know what the qualifications are. To begin with, there must be a knowledge of three foreign languages, French, German and Italian, and the capacity and will to endure great privation, suffering and, perhaps, death.'

'I was educated abroad, I can speak German and French. I do not know much Italian, but when I reach Italy I will soon learn.'

'Pardon me for asking you what may appear a rude question. Is it a personal disappointment which sends you to me, or love for the cause? It is not uncommon to find that young women, when earthly love is impossible, attempt to satisfy their cravings with a love for that which is impersonal.'

'Does it make any difference, so far as their constancy is concerned?'

'I cannot say that it does. The devotion of many of the martyrs of the Catholic church was repulsion from the world as much as attraction to heaven. You must understand that I am not prompted by curiosity. If you are to be my friend, it is necessary that I should know you thoroughly.'

'My motive is perfectly pure.'

They had some further talk and parted. After a few more interviews, Clara and another English lady started for Italy. Madge had letters from her sister at intervals for eighteen months, the last being from Venice. Then they ceased, and shortly afterwards Mazzini told Baruch that his sister-in-law was dead. All efforts to obtain more information from Mazzini were in vain, but one day when her name was mentioned, he said to Madge, –

'The theologians represent the Crucifixion as the most sublime fact in the world's history. It was sublime, but let us reverence also the Eternal Christ who is for ever being crucified for our salvation.'

'Father,' said a younger Clara to Baruch some ten years later as she sat on his knee, 'I had an Aunt Clara once, hadn't I?'

'Yes, my child.'

'Didn't she go to Italy and die there?'

'Yes.'

'Why did she go?'

'Because she wanted to free the poor people of Italy who were slaves.'

NOTES

---

p. 3 Eastthorpe . . . Fenmarket: fictional locations in the Fen country. Rutherford declines here to describe Eastthorpe having already done so in *Catharine Furze*, the novel that precedes *Clara Hopgood*. This implicit reference back to the earlier work suggests two things: firstly, that the situation of Madge and Clara ought to be compared with that of *Catharine Furze*; and secondly, that Rutherford assumes the novels are being read one by one, in the order of their composition, and that the reader is comparing one book with the other. The Fen country in Rutherford's writing is the flat, low-lying areas of land in Bedfordshire and neighbouring counties.

p. 3 There is, for example . . . interrupted by broken country: passages such as this one occur throughout Rutherford's novels. The natural world and the sky and stars function, to use Rutherford's own words, as a kind of 'corrective' to the 'littleness' that he felt was 'all around me' (*Autobiography*, Chapter 3). 'No man', he writes, 'can look up to the stars at night and reflect upon what lies behind them without feeling that the tyranny of the senses is loosened, and the tyranny, too, of the conclusions of his logic' (*Deliverance*, Chapter 6). William Hale White (WHW) believed that a realisation of the precision of the universe and of the individual's certain place within its organisation, could bring both consolation and liberation from an existence that might sometimes seem incomprehensible in its apparent triviality. This idea owes much to Spinoza who sought to present a vision of humanity simultaneously bound by necessity and externally free.

p. 3 Clara and Madge . . . playing chess: the conversation between the two women over the game shows the difference in their characters. Madge is the more intuitive in making initial judgements, pausing to reflect only afterwards; Clara deliberates before acting. What appears here to be a simple division between reason and impulse, is shown by the close of the novel to be much more complex. The irony is that 'rational' Clara doesn't win the game.

p. 4 1844: *Clara Hopgood* was first published in 1896 but Rutherford sets his narrative in 1844, making the sisters' conduct even more unconventional. The use of retrospect in Rutherford's novels functions as a means of showing how the pressure for change has its roots in the need of individuals to achieve personal freedom. All of the novels are about people who suffer because they are born into the 'wrong' time.

p. 6 Weimar: a small independent state in east Germany, centre of German enlightenment. Home of Goethe (1749–1832) and Schiller (1759–1805). WHW visited Weimar in June 1890.

p. 7 High and Low Church controversy: between 1833 and 1855 many members of the High Church (which emphasized the Catholic nature of the Church of England, stressed the authority of Church *and* Scripture, and attributed greater importance to the sacraments and priesthood) redefined their doctrinal stance, becoming 'Tractarians' and 'Anglo-Catholics'. In response, some members of the old Low Church tradition (who emphasized the essentially Protestant nature of the Church of England and placed special importance upon the authority of Scripture) became more self-consciously 'Evangelical'. Until the 1830s these different groups, though distinct, had managed to co-exist as part of a broad consensus within the Church of England. Their controversies force each party to define itself.

p. 8 Dr Dodderidge: Philip Dodderidge (1702–51), nonconformist minister. Doddridge's *Family Expositor*, a didactic commentary on the New Testament, first appeared in 1739. Between 1739 and 1756 six volumes of the *Expositor* were published.

p. 8 Matthew Henry: (1622–1714), nonconformist divine and minister. Henry's *Exposition of the New Testament*, first published in 1708, was followed by four more volumes. These were collected in a uniform volume in 1710.

p. 8 Reverend William Jay of Bath: (1768–1853), dissenting minister. Between 1842 and 1848 Jay published a collected edition of his writings in 12 volumes which included: 'The Mutual Duties of Husbands and

Wives' (1801); 'Short Discourses to be read in Families' (1805); and 'Morning Exercises in the Closet' (1829).

p. 9 vessels of wrath: Romans, 9:22.

p. 12 Thüringer Wald: a wooded mountain range in Thüringer, eastern Germany.

p. 13 *Egmont*: overture and nine items of incidental music, opus 84, composed in 1809–10 by Ludwig van Beethoven (1770–1827), to Goethe's drama about the Flemish aristocrat who defied Philip of Spain and was beheaded in 1567.

p. 13 *Fidelio*: *Fidelio oder Die eheliche Liebe* (*Fidelio, or Married Love*), opera by Beethoven to libretto by Josef Sonnleitner. Based on Bouilly's *Leonore, on L'Amour Conjugal*, first performed in Vienna in 1805.

p. 13 *Leben Jesu*: *Das Leben Jesu, kritisch bearbeitet*, 1835–6 (*The Life of Jesus critically examined*), most famous work of the German Biblical critic David Friedrich Strauss (1808–74). George Eliot translated the work into English in 1846, it was her first published work.

p. 14 Ottery St Mary: a market town in Devon, approximately 10km north of Sidmouth; birthplace of Samuel Taylor Coleridge.

p. 14 Corn Law: a series of laws passed in England from the 15th century onwards to protect agriculture by keeping the price of imported grain high. As England became industrialized, the Corn Laws came under increasing attack, notably from the Anti-Corn Law League, founded in Manchester in 1839. Their repeal by Sir Robert Peel in 1846 marked the triumph of free trade over protection (see also note to p. 104 below).

p. 14 Colonel Thompson: General T. Perronet Thompson (1788–1869), soldier and politician. In 1827 Thompson published the first version of his popular *Catechism of the Corn Laws*. This pamphlet, written in a racy style and full of humorous illustration, which purported to be written by a member of the university of Cambridge, was described as 'one of the most masterly and pungent exposures of fallacies' ever published.

p. 19 Mr Maurice: Frederick Denison Maurice (1805–72), Christian Socialist. Educated at Trinity Hall, Cambridge, Maurice joined the Church of England in 1830 and was ordained in 1834. In 1836 he became chaplain at Guy's Hospital where he was involved in advancing education. *The Kingdom of Christ*, his most enduring work and a plea for Christian unity, was published in 1838. Two years later he was elected Professor of English Literature and History at King's College, London. In 1848 he was associated in the foundation of Queen's College, London, the first higher education establishment for women. Maurice's involvement with the Christian Socialist movement brought him into contact with Charles Kingsley (author of *The Water Babies* and *Alton Locke*). In 1853 *Theological Essays* was published, and in the same year Maurice's unorthodox views on eternal punishment led to his dismissal from King's College (where he was responsible for the instruction of ordinands). He went on to found a working man's college in 1854 and was its first principal. In 1859 he published *What is Revelation?* His appointment in 1866 as Professor of Moral Philosophy at Cambridge is a measure of the increasing tolerance of 'broad' views.

p. 19 Mr Sterling: John Sterling (1806–44), author. A leading member of the 'Apostles' club and friend of Francis Newman; with F. D. Maurice, Sterling was briefly proprietor of the *Athenaeum* in 1828. He contributed to various periodicals, including *Blackwoods*. Among his published works are a novel *Arthur Coningsby* (1833), *Poems* (1839), and *Essays and Tales* (1848).

p. 22 St Paul: oratorio by Felix Mendlessohn (1809–47).

p. 23 C *minor* Symphony: Beethoven's symphony no. 5 in C minor, opus 67. Composed 1804–8, first performed in Vienna.

p. 24 *Adelaide*: song by Beethoven (opus 46) for soprano and piano. Composed 1794–5, to a poem by F. Von Matthisson.

p. 31 orrery: a clockwork model of the planetary system, named after the Earl of Orrery (*c.* 1700), see note to p. 3 above.

p. 33 *Il mio Tesoro*: solo aria from the opera *Don Giovanni* (*The Rake Punished*). Composed in 1787 by Wolfgang Amadeus Mozart

(1756–91), to a libretto by Da Ponte. Based on the Don Juan legend as told in Bertati.

p. 33 *Destruction of Sennacherib*: poem by Lord Byron (1788–1824), published in *Hebrew Melodies Ancient and Modern* (1815).

p. 33 Sir Henry Wooton's *Happy Life*: Henry Wooton (1568–1639) was a traveller, diplomat, scholar and poet. Educated at Winchester and Oxford (where he met John Donne), Wooton became the confidant of the Earl of Essex. When Essex fell from favour, Wooton fled first to France, then Italy and was sent by Ferdinand Duke of Florence on a secret mission to James VI of Scotland. James later knighted Wooton and sent him as ambassador to Venice in 1604 where he remained for 20 years. He returned to England a poor man in 1614, was made provost of Eton and took orders. 'The Character of a Happy Life' was printed in 1614.

p. 33 The scene . . . playing chess: *Tempest*, V.i.

p. 34 *Zampa*: opera by Ferdinand Herold (1791–1833). Herold composed some of the most enduring masterpieces in the genre *Opera comique*, popular throughout the nineteenth century. The subject of *Zampa* is the reverse of the Don Juan legend. Zampa the pirate dies in the arms of a marble statue after placing a wedding ring on its finger in jest. The statue is the image of a young girl deceived in love and deserted.

p. 34 'Behold . . . Prospero': *Tempest*, V.i.107–8.

p. 34 'Sir . . . mine': *Tempest*, V.i.187–88.

p. 35 Gonzalo . . . on the couple: *Tempest*, V.i.199–203.

p. 37 'Sweet lord . . . not for the world': *Tempest*, V.i.172–4.

p. 40 'The long brook . . . to the sea': ll. 8–9 of *Oenone*, a poem by Alfred Tennyson (1809–92), published in 1832 and revised for 1842. In Greek mythology Oenone was a nymph of Mount Ida who married Paris and was deserted by him for Helen.

p. 40 'Behind the valley . . . the morning': *Oenone*, ll. 10–11.

p. 43 *Intimations of Immortality*: *Intimations of Immortality from Recollections of Early Childhood*, poem by William Wordsworth (1770–1850), first published in 1907. The poem was originally entitled 'Ode' and the motto was 'Paulo majora canamus' ('Let us sing a little higher'). From 1815 onwards the poem carried the title that Rutherford alludes to in his abbreviation. Like Madge, WHW, though a great admirer of Wordsworth, disliked the poem. He wrote that 'It is desultory, will not stand examination ... by the reason' (*Athenaeum*, 3648, 25 September 1897) 412.

p. 43 'And custom lie ... almost as life!': *Intimations of Immortality*, 11. 58–9.

p. 45 **Frankfort O.M.**: Frankfurt am Main (west Germany), as opposed to Frankfurt an der Oder (east Germany).

p. 49 **Myddleton Square, Pentonville**: Myddleton Square was a new and affluent development within the more downmarket Pentonville which had been built in the 1720s by Alderman Penton.

p. 51 *Kyrie* from Beethoven's Mass in C: *Kyrie eleison* (Lord have mercy), an invocation used in Church of England, Roman Catholic and Greek Orthodox Churches, especially at the beginning of mass.

p. 51 **St Mary's, Moorfields**: a large Catholic Church in London, built before Westminster cathedral.

p. 54 **She never ... dissenting chapel**: Dissenters is a general term for Presbyterians, Baptists, Congregationalists, Quakers and other Protestants dissenting from, and failing to conform to the restored Church of England in 1662. The chapel is a place of Nonconformist worship; the use of the word chapel distinguishes Nonconformists from the wider church-going community.

p. 55 **Mrs Caffyn ... St Paul**: see Paul's Epistle to the Romans, 4:5; 5:1 and the Epistle of James, 2:17: 'Even so faith, if it hath not works, is dead, being alone'.

p. 61 **mechanic's institute**: voluntary organizations formed between 1820 and 1869 to educate manual workers. Forerunners of the mechanic's institute included the Birmingham Brotherly Society (1797), and the London Institute for Diffusion of Science, Medicine, and the Arts (1809). The London Mechanic's Institute was founded in 1823. By 1860 the number of these organizations ran into hundreds.

p. 62 Chartism: the campaign for democratic rights which swept across Britain in 1838 and 39. A series of demonstrations in 1838, including one of over 100,000 in Manchester, and the collection of one and a half million signatures, culminated in the first Chartist Petition to Parliament in 1839. In July 1840 the National Charter Organization was formed, the movement was founded on a six point People's Charter which included demands for universal (male) suffrage, annual parliaments, vote by secret ballot, abolition of the property qualification for MPs, and equal electoral districts. This was the first working-class political movement in Britain and by the time that the second petition was presented in 1842, the N.C.A. claimed to have established more than 400 branches with over 40,000 members.

p. 63 She did all she could . . . the child died: the idea that women possess an 'energy' for exercise which is exclusively expressed in motherhood and domestic work is first made explicit in *Miriam's Schooling* and is reiterated in *Catharine Furze* in a passage that foreshadows the one above: 'The force in woman is so great that something on which it can grapple, in which it can expend itself, is a necessity, and Catharine felt that her strength would have to occupy itself twisting straws. It is really this which is the root of many a poor girl's suffering. As the world is arranged at present, there is too much power for the mills which have to be turned by it' (*Catharine Furze*, Chapter 17).

One of the first things we learn about Madge and Clara Hopgood is that their father had anticipated the danger that Rutherford presents in *Miriam's Schooling* and *Catharine Furze*. Mr Hopgood maintained that girls 'even more than boys' needed a good education, in order to avoid the 'disease' that 'untutored thoughts' can 'breed' in unmarried girls (*Clara Hopgood*, p. 5). Clearly, Mr Hopgood sees the possibility that marriage might not be the destiny of his daughters.

p. 67 *The Three Ravens*: Joseph Ritson in his *Ancient Songs and Ballads From the Reign of King Henry the Second* (London: Reeves and Turner, 1877) describes *The Three Ravens* as a dirge from Ravenscroft's 'Melismata. Musical Phantasies. Fitting the Cittie, and Countrey Humours. To 3,4, and 5 Voyces', where it is inserted under the head of 'Countrey Pastimes'. This ballad is not only much older than the date of the book (1611), but than most of the other pieces contained in it. Rutherford quotes the final verse of the ballad.

p. 68 for who . . . his stature? echo of Matthew, 6:28.

p. 69 the Athanasian Creed: one of the three ecumenical creeds widely used in Western Christendom as a profession of orthodox faith. WHW 'objected' to the Athanasian Creed because he felt that it encouraged 'the belief that religion is an intellectual subtlety', this he thought to be 'mischievous' (*Letters to Three Friends*, p. 231).

p. 74 Madge recognised . . . St Ann's fugue: fugue in e flat by Johann Sebastian Bach (1685–1750) for organ, published in 1739. The fugue is named after the saint because it resembles an English hymn tune to her.

p. 74 Baruch Cohen, a mathematical instrument maker: Cohen shares the same forename as the seventeenth century Jewish philosopher, Baruch or Benedict Spinoza (1632–77), some of whose works WHW translated. Baruch is the Hebrew form of the Latin Benedict ('blessed'). Spinoza was a lens grinder; Cohen a mathematical instrument maker, both of which require precise measurement and absolute accuracy. Spinoza's philosophical arguments are presented in the form of geometrical theorems: he supplies Definitions and Axioms from which he derives Propositions, Proofs and Corollaries. Mathematics also forms the 'foundation' (*Clara Hopgood*, p. 126) of Cohen's 'philosophy'. It is through the character of Cohen that the thoughts of Spinoza are mediated in the novel.

Spinoza inspired many of the nineteenth-century's most profound thinkers, amongst them Coleridge, George Eliot, G. H. Lewes, J. A. Froude and Matthew Arnold. Basil Willey calls Spinoza 'the first great saint of modern rationalism' (*More Nineteenth-Century Studies: A Group of Honest Doubters*, p. 117).

p. 75 Antares: a gigantic red star, over 250 times the diameter of the Sun, in the constellation of Scorpius. Its name, meaning 'rival of Mars', derives from its red tint, which resembles Mars.

p. 76 Manning and Bray's *History of Surrey*: Owen Manning and William Bray's *The History of the Antiquities of the County of Surrey*, published in 3 volumes by J. White (no relation to WHW) in London, between 1804–14.

p. 77 Dulwich and Denmark Hill Directory: a directory of traders, including potted histories and details of who lived where.

p. 79 *After Office Hours* **by a man named Robinson:** fictional work and author.

p. 79 *Heroes and Hero Worship*: *On Heroes, Hero-worship and the Heroic in History*, a course of six lectures delivered in 1840 and published in 1841, by Thomas Carlyle. In this work, Carlyle asserts that 'Universal History' is the 'History of ... Great Men'. Carlyle chooses as examples of such men Odin, Dante, Luther, Dr Johnson, Rousseau, Burns, Cromwell and Napoleon. Perhaps Rutherford has some idea of redressing Carlyle's gender bias in representing in the last three novels a 'History of Women' and by presenting Clara Hopgood as a hero.

   After Office Hours was supposedly published in the same year as *Heroes and Hero Worship*, that is, four years before the opening of the narrative of *Clara Hopgood*. This linking together of the fictional and actual is typical of Rutherford.

p. 80 Quakerism: Quakers were members of the Religious Society of Friends which grew out of the controversies of 1650 in England. The Friends were distinguished by pacifist principals, plainness of dress and manners, refusal to take oaths, faith in the Inner Light as the only way to Christ, and the absence of clergy or ministers. The Friends were known as Quakers, according to their founder George Fox, 'because I bid them, Tremble at the word of the Lord'.

p. 81 *Paradise Lost*: epic poem by John Milton (1608–74) first published in 1667. It takes as its subject the disobedience of Adam and Eve and their expulsion from Eden.

p. 95 **Mr A. J. Scott**: Alexander John Scott (1805–66), first principal of Owen's College. Graduating from the University of Glasgow in 1827, Scott was licenced to preach in the Church of Scotland. In 1828 he met Thomas and Edward Irving and the latter invited him to be his assistant in London. In 1830 Scott received an invitation to the pastorate of the Scottish Church at Woolwich, the necessary ordination involved assent to the Westminster Confession (one of the most influential creeds of Calvinism) which Scott could not give. He thought it his duty to embody his objections in a letter to the moderator of the London presbytery. He was subsequently charged with heresy in May 1831 and deprived of his licence to preach. In 1848 he obtained the chair of English Language and Literature at University College, London. With the Reverend Gaskell and others, Scott played a part in founding the Manchester Working Men's College (now the University of Manchester), to which he was appointed principal in 1851.

p. 96 **Few men understand ... they know nothing**: it may be that Rutherford is referring here to the real life friendship between WHW and the Welsh preacher and mystic, Caleb Morris (1800–65). Morris preached at Fetter Lane Chapel and Eccleston Square Chapel in London between 1830 and 1850. Having heard some of the finest speakers of his day, including Cobden, Bright, Gladstone and Binney, WHW was convinced that Morris was the most eloquent man he knew. A few lines later, Baruch refers explicitly to 'a young Welshman ... who is a perfect orator' (p. 96).

p. 96 **Thomas À Kempis**: German mystic (c. 1380–1471). À Kempis entered the Augustinian convent of Mt Saint Agnes near Zwolle and was ordained priest in 1413. All of his writings are of a devotional nature, but his fame rests upon *De imitatione Christi et contemptu omnium vanitatum mundi* (*The Imitation of Christ*), which traces in four books the gradual progress of the soul to Christian perfection.

p. 98 **Ranmore Common, Camilla Lacy ... who once lived there?**: Camilla Lacy is the name of a house in Surrey to the north-east of Ranmore Common and due west of Westhumble, just off the Dorking Road (A24). The house belonged to the writer Fanny Burney (1752–1840) and was purchased with the proceeds from her novel

Camilla (1796). The house and most of its contents burnt down in 1919. Burney's three major novels, *Evelina* (1778), *Cecilia* (1782) and *Camilla*, take as their theme the emergence of a young, intelligent but inexperienced woman into the world, where she is exposed to circumstances that form her character.

p. 99 The recognition ... Socrates: Rutherford is here expressing something like what Spinoza called the 'intellectual love of God'. In the Preface to the Second Edition of Spinoza's *Ethic*, WHW says 'In so far as the mind is capable of intellectual love it is not only eternal but part of God himself'. Some commentaries on Spinoza's metaphysics regard personal love as the most adequate expression of this union. Cf. *Clara Hopgood*, Chapter 24: 'Baruch was now in love .... "No man," said Baruch once "can love a woman unless he loves God." "I should say," smilingly replied the Gentile, "that no man can love God unless he loves a woman." "I am right," said Baruch, "and so are you."'

p. 102 *Moreh Nevochim* of Maimonides: Moses Maimonides (1135–1204) was a leading Jewish philosopher of the Middle Ages. In the *Moreh Nevochim* (*Guide to the Perplexed*), Maimonides seeks to show that though God cannot be known, he can be appreciated and worshipped through an acquaintance with his workings in the natural order. For Maimonides, Revelation has the role of educating the believer to know God in knowing nature and not of imparting distinctive truths. The *Guide*, in addition to being a fundamental text of medieval Jewish thought, exercised an influence on medieval discussions of the relation between faith and reason.

p. 102 a greater than Maimonides: Spinoza.

p. 104 Free Trade Meeting: in this context a meeting organised by the Anti-Corn Law League (see second note to p. 14 above). This very effective association was formed in 1838 and by 1839 had become a national organization. Its main orators were John Bright and Richard Cobden. The Free Trade Hall in Manchester was built to accommodate Free Trade meetings and had a capacity of 8–9,000.

p. 112 a mass of Mozart's: *The New Grove Dictionary of Music and*

Musicians lists several masses by Mozart, including *Missa solemnis, Missa brevis* and *Missa longa.*

p. 112 **Henry Vincent** (1813–78), Chartist agitator. In 1828, Vincent was apprenticed to a printer in Hull. On termination of his apprenticeship he moved with his family to London. He was the chief speaker at the Great Chartist meeting held in London at the end of 1838. He was arrested, tried and sentenced to twelve months' imprisonment in 1839 for offences related to his activities as a Chartist. His imprisonment was the cause of an armed rising in attempt to secure his release, during which ten rioters were killed. Vincent was again imprisoned in 1840 and it was after his release that he married and settled at Bath, where he and his wife published the *Vindicator*. Vincent stood for election eight times but on all occasions was defeated. His long career as a public lecturer began soon after his marriage with addresses on such issues as 'The Constitutional History of the Parliaments', 'Home Life: its Duties and Pleasures', and 'The Working Classes of the World: their Social and Political Rights and Duties'. Vincent's religious sympathies were with the Society of Friends (see note to p. 80 above), though he was never a member. He frequently conducted services on Sundays among the free churches as a lay preacher.

p. 113 ***Northern Star:*** a leading Chartist newspaper founded in 1837 by Feargus O'Connor. The *Northern Star* represented the more radical wing of Chartism and gained a substantial circulation (50,000), mainly among the working-class in northern towns.

p. 114 **the stockingers in Leicester:** the stocking weavers of Leicester. As early as 1740 'as poor as a stockinger' had become a proverbial expression. Until the second half of the nineteenth century, Leicester had one large scale industry, the manufacture of hosiery. By the end of The Napoleonic Wars a depression had developed in the hosiery industry that was to be almost permanent until the coming of the modern factories. From 1810 onwards, with the increasing substitution of trousers for breeches, a blow was dealt to the industry which did not make up on socks what it lost on stockings.

p. 114 **God made the man – man made the slave:** final line of a hymn written by John Bramwich (*c.* 1792–1846), a Leicester stocking-weaver, first published in Thomas Cooper's weekly *Extinguisher* and later collected, along with thirteen others of Bramwich's composition, in the *Shakespearean Chartist Hymn Book*. The hymn was sung to the hymn tune 'New Crucifixion'. Bramwich had been a soldier and had seen service in the West Indies and in America; he died of exhaustion from hard labour and want, aged 54.

p. 117 Whenever Mrs Caffyn talked ... art, poetry, and philosophy seem little better than trifling: in December 1899, disgusted at the lack of justification for the Boer War, WHW wrote to his friend, Miss Partridge: 'A more cowardly Government than this Government never existed, and it *therefore* bullies the Boers.' Under such circumstances, he goes on, 'All art, literature, seem to me a mockery now – mere trifling' (*Letters to Three Friends*, p. 193). A similar sentiment is expressed in 'An Apology', *Pages from a Journal*, pp. 78–82.

p. 118 Shelley's *Revolt of Islam*: 'A poem in Twelve Cantos' by Percy Bysshe Shelley (1792–1822). Composed in 1817 and printed with the title *Laon and Cythna; or, The Revolution of the Golden City: A Vision of the Nineteenth Century*, the poem was suppressed by the publishers, pending revision. In January 1818 it was published, with fresh title page as *The Revolt of Islam*.

p. 119 Rollin's *Ancient History*: Charles Rollin, French historian (1661–1741), *Histoire ancienne des Egyptiens, des Carthaginois, des Assyriens, des Babyloniens, des Medes, et des Perses, des Macedoniens, des Grecs*, published in Paris, 1730–38.

The *Ancient History* was translated into English 1738-40. The eighteenth edition, revised, corrected and illustrated with maps in 6 volumes, was published by Thomas Tegg in London in 1839.

p. 119 *Fabricius, J. A. Bibliothecha Ecclesiastica in qua continentur*: John Albert Fabricius (1668–1736). The British Library Catalogue lists *Bibliotheca Ecclesiastica in qua continentur*. It also lists *S. Basilii Caesareae Cappadociae Archiepiscopi opera omnia quae exstant*.

p. 122 Mazzini: Giuseppe Mazzini (1805–72), Italian patriot, born at Genoa. In 1831 Mazzini addressed an appeal to Charles Albert of

Piedmont, urging him to put himself at the head of the struggle for
Italian independence; the answer, under Metternich's influence, was a
sentence of perpetual banishment. The following year the French
authorities expelled him from France. In 1834 he organized an abortive
invasion of Savoy. Banished from Switzerland in 1836, he found refuge
in London in 1837. Leghorn received him with enthusiasm in February
1849, just before the republic was proclaimed at Rome, where in
March Mazzini, Saffi and Armellini were appointed a triumvirate with
dictatorial powers. The following month the French arrived at Rome
and after a struggle the republic fell. From London Mazzini planned
the attempted risings at Mantua (1852), Milan (1853), Genoa (1857)
and Leghorn (1857). Mazzini died at Pisa in 1872. He saw Italy united
but not, as he would have hoped, as a republic.

p. 129 just as he ... emerald to look upon: Revelation of St John,
4:2–4.

SUGGESTIONS FOR FURTHER READING

Most writing on the work of Mark Rutherford concentrates on the first two novels: *The Autobiography of Mark Rutherford* (1881) and *Mark Rutherford's Deliverance* (1881). The third novel, *The Revolution in Tanner's Lane* (1887), has attracted some comment, mostly for what is thought to be its faulty structure or the supposed inaccuracy of its portrayal of Dissent. The later novels, significantly those which take women as their central figures (*Miriam's Schooling* [1890], *Catharine Furze* [1893], *Clara Hopgood* [1896], have had virtually no serious scholarly attention. For this reason my reading list includes studies of Rutherford's work generally.

Contemporary Reviews of Clara Hopgood

Academy, 15 August 1896.

Athenaeum, 15 August 1896.

Critic, 15 August 1896.

Nation (New York), 3 September 1896.

Studies of Mark Rutherford in Books and Journals

Massingham, H. W., 'Memorial Introduction', *The Autobiography of Mark Rutherford* (London: T. Fisher Unwin, 1923).

Baker, E. A., 'Mark Rutherford and Others', *The History of the English Novel*, 10 vols (London: Riverside Press, 1938) IX, 97–121 (p. 97).

Maclean, Catherine Macdonald, *Mark Rutherford: A Biography of William Hale White* (London: Macdonald, 1955).

Stock, Irvin, *William Hale White (Mark Rutherford): A Critical Study* (London: Unwin, 1956).

Stone, W. H., 'The Confessional Fiction of Mark Rutherford', *University of Toronto Quarterly*, 25 (1956), pp. 35–57.

——'Hale White and George Eliot', *University of Toronto Quarterly*, 25 (1956), pp. 437–51.

Willey, Basil, 'Mark Rutherford', *More Nineteenth Century Studies: A Group of Honest Doubters* (New York: Columbus Press, 1965), pp. 185–247.

Salgado, Gamini, 'The Rhetoric of Sincerity: *The Autobiography of Mark Rutherford* as Fiction', *Renaissance and Modern Essays Presented to Vivian de Sola Pinto in celebration of his seventieth birthday*, ed. G. R. Hibbard (London: Routledge & Kegan Paul, 1966), pp. 159–68.

Daiches, David, *Some Late Victorian Attitudes* (London: André Deutsch, 1969), pp. 91–123.

Hughes, Linda, 'Madge and Clara Hopgood: William Hale White's Spinozan Sisters', *Victorian Studies*, 18 (1974), 57–75.

Cunningham, Valentine, *Everywhere Spoken Against: Dissent in the Victorian Novel* (Oxford: Clarendon, 1975).

Tomalin, Claire, 'Maggie Tulliver's little sisters', *The Listener*, 94, 16 October 1975, pp. 515–17.

Merton, Stephen, *Mark Rutherford (William Hale White)* (New York: Twayne Publishers, 1976).

Lucas, John, 'William Hale White and the Problems of Deliverance', *The Literature of Change: Studies in the Nineteenth-Century Provincial Novel* (New York: Barnes and Noble, 1977), pp. 57–113.

Allen, Peter, 'Mark Rutherford: The Anatomy of a Failure', *The View from the Pulpit: Victorian Ministers and Society* (Canada: Macmillan, 1978).

Swann, Charles, 'The Author of "Mark Rutherford", or, Who Wrote *Miriam's Schooling*?', *Yearbook of English Studies*, 9 (1979), pp. 270–78.

Brookes, Gerry H., 'Fictional Forms in William Hale White's *Autobiography of Mark Rutherford* and *Mark Rutherford's Deliverance*', *Biography: An Interdisciplinary Quarterly* (1986) vol. 9, part 3, pp. 247–68.

Grossman, Anita S., 'William Hale White and the example of George
Eliot', *Papers on Language and Literature*, 24 (1988), pp. 159–76.
Harland, Catherine R., *Mark Rutherford: The Mind and Art of William
Hale White* (Columbus: Ohio State University Press, 1988).
Goode, John, 'Mark Rutherford and Spinoza', *English Literature in
Transition*, 34 (1991), pp. 424–53.

The Works of Mark Rutherford
(William Hale White)

The Autobiography of Mark Rutherford: Dissenting Minister (1881).
*Mark Rutherford's Deliverance: Being the Second Part of his Autobiog-
raphy* (1885).
The Revolution in Tanner's Lane (1887).
Miriam's Schooling (1890).
Catharine Furze (1893).
John Bunyan (1895).
Clara Hopgood (1896).
Pages from a Journal: with other papers (1900).
More Pages from a Journal (1910).
The Early Life of Mark Rutherford (W. Hale White) By Himself
(1913).

Works Published in William Hale White's Name

*An Argument for an Extension of the Franchise: A Letter addressed to
George Jacob Holyoake Esq.* (1866).
A Letter Written on the Death of Mrs Elizabeth Street (1877).
An Examination of the Charge of Apostasy against Wordsworth
(1898).

Works Translated, Edited and Prefaced by
William Hale White

Ethic: Translated from the Latin of Benedict Spinoza (1883).
Tractatus: Translated from the Latin of Benedict Spinoza (1895).

William White, *The Inner Life of the House of Commons* (1897), introduction by William Hale White.

A Description of the Wordsworth and Coleridge Manuscripts in the possession of Mr T. Norton Longman (1987), ed. William Hale White.

Coleridge's Poems: A Facsimile Reproduction of the Proofs and MSS. of Some of the Poems (1899), preface and notes by William Hale White.

Selections from Dr Johnson's 'Rambler' (1907), introduction by William Hale White.

Works Edited by Dorothy Vernon White

Last Pages from a Journal (1915).
Letters to Three Friends (1923).
The Groombridge Diary (1924).

TEXT SUMMARY

The novel opens in 1844, in the provincial town of Fenmarket. Since the death of their father, Madge and Clara Hopgood have lived with their mother in genteel but straitened circumstances. Mr Hopgood believed that girls, even more than boys, benefit from a good education. Consequently Madge and Clara have been to school in Weimar.

Frank Palmer, a salesman travelling for his father's firm, has visited Fenmarket several times and has often noticed Madge. Having made enquiries about her, he learns that her father and his had been best friends. Anxious to know more of her, Frank obtains a letter of introduction from his father which he presents to Mrs Hopgood. He becomes a regular visitor at the Hopgoods' whenever business calls him to Fenmarket and, in time, Frank's brief trips are extended: the society of the Hopgood women, rather than business, draws him to the town – in particular that of Madge.

On one of his visits, during a walk in the country, Frank displays remarkable courage by distracting a charging ox from its pursuit of the party. The act is decisive: Madge is convinced that Frank has saved her life. Frank is in love with Madge.

A grand entertainment is planned in Fenmarket. Madge and Frank contribute; Frank with a song and Madge with a recitation. They are such a success that a local dignitary invites them to perform at a party at her home. Madge and Frank act out a scene from *The Tempest*; Madge as Miranda and Frank as Ferdinand. The couple are again vigorously applauded even though, as Clara hints, there is much less acting in their performance than might have been necessary.

It has always been understood by Mr Palmer and his son that Frank should be sent abroad to work. Mr Palmer delays Frank's trip until the summer because since meeting Madge Frank has become less enthusiastic about this plan. Postponement allows Madge and Frank to spend more time together and they become engaged. Clara suspects that

Madge has reservations about Frank which Madge is reluctant to recognise. Madge feels Clara's fears and a reserve develops between the sisters.

The time comes for Frank to leave England. He spends a final Sunday at Fenmarket. Whilst out walking alone, a storm develops and Madge and Frank are obliged to take shelter in a barn. They make love. Afterwards Frank is stricken with shame and fear and feels that he cannot now go abroad. Madge insists that there should be no alteration to his plans and he leave the next morning for Germany. He writes to Madge, full of remorse about their intimacy and begging forgiveness. He urges Madge to allow him to return so that they can marry immediately. Madge is resolute: the relationship is over, Frank need not return, there is no need of forgiveness, he must not write to her again. Frank does write again but the letter remains unopened. He is tormented by the fear that Madge might be pregnant and the scandal this would cause.

Madge gives no explanation to her mother or Clara for the termination of her engagement. Two months later she tells her mother she is pregnant. Mrs Hopgood is at first shocked but soon accepts the situation as irrevocable.

The three women move to Pentonville, London, but it soon depresses them. Madge is made more miserable by the thought that she is the primary cause of her mother's and sister's unhappiness. One morning, very low inspirits, she sets out on a long walk that takes her beyond Letherhead. Exhausted, Madge rests in a church porch, where she is noticed by an old woman, Mrs Caffyn. Mrs Caffyn realises that Madge is upset, unwell, pregnant and wears no wedding ring. She convinces Madge that she should not try to return home that evening but should accompany her to Great Oakhurst where, having sent word to her family, she can spend the night. Madge returns to London the next morning.

Mrs Hopgood is given notice to quit the lodgings because the landlady, Mrs Cork, fears that retaining the Hopgoods as her tenants will damage her reputation. Madge's condition, as well as her absence from home the previous night, are cited as evidence that the family are not respectable and as just cause for eviction. Mrs Hopgood tells her daughters that they must leave, but does not explain why. She travels to Great Oakhurst to thank Mrs Caffyn for her kindness to Madge. On the journey home Mrs Hopgood has to ride outside the coach in pouring rain. The following morning she informs her daughters that they will be moving to Great Ormond Street where they will stay with Mrs Caffyn's daughter, Mrs Marshall. Mrs Hopgood develops inflammation of the lungs: a week later she is dead. Without their mother's annuity, Clara and Madge are left with only seventy-five pounds a year to support themselves.

Frank Palmer writes again to Fenmarket. The letter is forwarded to the Hopgoods' first London lodging and returned unopened to Frank. He realises that the Hopgoods have moved, intuits why and returns to England straightaway. In Pentonville he is told by Mrs Cork that the Hopgoods' new address is not known.

That evening, at his father's house, there is a musical party. Despite his depression Frank attends and renews his acquaintance with his cousin Cecilia. They sing together and Frank is hard pressed to restrain himself from admiring her. They pledge to sing together again soon and Frank presents Cecilia with a blood red begonia. When the party is over Frank's thoughts return to Madge and to what he believes must be his duty.

Returning to the Pentonville lodging the next morning Frank is told by Mrs Cork's maid that the Hopgoods have gone to Great Ormond Street. His scrutiny of the street for some sign of his friends is unsuccessful.

At church on Sunday Cecilia reminds him of his promise to sing with her, and, during the course of their duet and other conversation that evening, the cousins are drawn much closer. Though his thoughts are full of Cecilia, when he is alone Frank is once again stricken with guilt about Madge. He determines to make one last effort to contact her before returning to Germany.

Stationing himself at one end of Great Ormond Street early next morning, Frank sees Madge leaving one of the houses. He approaches her and although she at first refuses to listen to him, they go to St Paul's where they are able to talk. Frank implores Madge to take him back but she is adamantly against it. She expects nothing from him and will have nothing more to do with him.

If the sisters are to manage financially, Clara must find work to supplement their income. Mr Marshall, husband of their landlady, mentions to his brother-in-law Baruch Cohen that Clara is in search of work. Cohen knows of a bookseller in need of a clerk and, on his recommendation, Clara is given the job. Cohen calls at the bookshop. Usually reticent – a lonely man and a widower – he is amazed to find it very easy to talk to Clara.

Madge has become a particular favourite with Mrs Caffyn, whose affection easily extends to her baby girl when she is born. Mrs Caffyn urges Madge to think again about Frank and Madge is moved momentarily by her protestations. Madge's resolve soon returns: she cannot marry Frank. Mrs Caffyn decides to write to Frank herself.

Frank receives Mrs Caffyn's letter and responds with two of his own: one to Mrs Caffyn and one to Madge. In the former he explains that pressing engagements prevent his immediate return to London, enclosing £20 which he hopes Mrs Caffyn will contrive to convey to Madge. In the latter he pleads to be allowed to do his duty by his child and its mother. Madge remains unmoved by his pleas. Mrs Caffyn returns the money along with a brief note expressing her relief that he had not, after all, been able to see Madge.

Cohen is curious about Clara and Madge. He visits the bookshop again and speaks to Clara alone. Both she and Cohen, reflecting upon their conversation, are astonished by its range and by their mutual lack of reserve. Some weeks later Cohen calls at the Marshalls' house where he talks to Clara again and learns more about Madge from Mrs Caffyn. Cohen has fallen in love with Clara and she loves him in return, though there has been no declaration.

Frank Palmer returns to England disturbed by Mrs Caffyn's last letter and Madge's continued refusal to communicate with him. At home he sings and practises with Cecilia. Both their families consider them to be a couple and they are soon married.

Cohen feels deeply for Clara, but he is anxious and hesitant about declaring himself. One evening, walking Clara home from the bookshop, it becomes clear to both of them, though without explicit acknowledgment, that some sort of declaration is on Cohen's lips. Clara deliberately cuts short their walk, thereby removing the opportunity for Cohen to speak, and he returns home alone and despondent.

A month later, Marshall invites Clara, Madge and Cohen to accompany him on a visit to the Italian revolutionary Mazzini, who is living in England under an assumed name. Clara asks him about the process of recruiting volunteers to his cause and is surprised to hear that well qualified women are considered of great use.

Clara arranges a weekend away for herself, Mrs Caffyn, Clara, Madge and her baby, Mr and Mrs Marshall and Cohen. She is restless and, taking a walk alone, she sees Cohen and Madge together in the distance. The whole party take a trip to Norbury where Madge and Cohen again go off alone together and Cohen proposes to her. She accepts. When the group is reassembled Madge takes Clara aside and tells her about the engagement. Clara is happy at the news.

Returning to London, Clara visits Mazzini and volunteers her help in his cause. He explains to her the grave risks involved and asks whether her decision has been promoted by a personal disappointment. Clara assures him that her motive is sound.

Clara leaves for Italy and corresponds with Madge at intervals. After eighteen months all communication ceases. Mazzini informs Cohen that Clara is dead.

ACKNOWLEDGEMENTS

I wish to acknowledge my debt to James Rand for introducing me to the work of 'Mark Rutherford' and for his advice on every aspect of this edition. I am grateful to Brian Nellist of the University of Liverpool for his guidance. Lesley Cullen deserves my thanks for her help in typing the editorial material. Finally, I must thank my youngest daughter, Jennie Holmes, for her patience and for the practical assistance she gave in the preparation of this edition.